PRINCETON STUDIES IN INTERNATIONAL FINANCE NO. 23

# The Fund Agreement:
# Living Law and Emerging Practice

by

Hans Aufricht

INTERNATIONAL FINANCE SECTION

DEPARTMENT OF ECONOMICS

PRINCETON UNIVERSITY

PRINCETON, NEW JERSEY

1969

Printed in the United States of America by Princeton University Press
at Princeton, New Jersey

# CONTENTS

# THE FUND AGREEMENT:
# LIVING LAW AND EMERGING PRACTICE

## I. THE FUND AGREEMENT—SOME GENERAL
## OBSERVATIONS

The Articles of Agreement of the International Monetary Fund (or the Fund Agreement), adopted at the Bretton Woods Conference[1] on July 22, 1944, entered into force on December 27, 1945.

The Fund Agreement[2] is the organic law of the IMF. It constitutes the legal basis of the structure and functions of the IMF. Up to now—October 1968—the Fund Agreement has never been formally amended, but it has been modified in various ways. The modifications of the Agreement can be traced back primarily to (1) interpretations of the Fund Agreement by the Fund, (2) changes in the structure of the Fund, and (3) rights and responsibilities of the Fund conferred on the Fund by other international agreements such as the General Agreement on Tariffs and Trade (GATT) and the General Arrangements to Borrow (GAB).

The first formal amendment of the Fund Agreement under Article XVII of the Agreement was recently proposed.[3] In this connection the question arises: What is to be amended, the Fund Agreement as originally formulated at Bretton Woods or the Fund Agreement as modified in the period December 1945 through October 1968? To ignore the fact that during this period the Fund Agreement has been subject to significant modifications would be unrealistic. Clear insight into the legal framework within which the Fund operates presupposes

---

[1] For text of the Final Act and Related Documents, see *United Nations Monetary and Financial Conference, Bretton Woods, New Hampshire, July 1 to July 22, 1944*. Department of State Publication 2187, Conference Series 55 (Washington: 1944), hereafter cited as "Final Act."

[2] For text of the Fund Agreement, see Final Act, pp. 28-67. The Fund Agreement has also been published by the U.S. Department of State in pamphlet form as *Treaties and Other International Acts Series 1501*, Department of State Publication 2512 (Washington: 1946). Also the IMF has issued the Fund Agreement in pamphlet form with analytical Index (Seventh Printing, Washington: 1967)

[3] See IMF, *Proposed Amendment of Articles of Agreement: A Report by the Executive Directors to the Board of Governors* (Washington: April 1968), hereafter cited as the "April 1968 Report of the Executive Directors."

*1*

awareness of the living law of the Fund as it has evolved in the practice of the Fund in the course of 23 years of its existence. This study purports to provide a guide to the living law of the Fund under the following major headings: I. The Fund Agreement—Some General Observations; II. Interpretation of the Fund Agreement; III. The Drawing Rights of Members—Law and Policy; IV. The Fund Agreement and the Gold Standard; V. The Changing Setting; and VI. Retrospect and Prospect.

## 1. OFFICIAL LANGUAGE

The English version of the Fund Agreement is the official version. All members are required to sign the original copy of the Articles held in the Archives of the Government of the United States of America.[4] By signing the Agreement, the prospective member certifies that it is bound by the English version. This act of signature does not prohibit members from publishing the Fund Agreement *pro foro interno*, for example in the Official Gazette, in the official language or languages of the country. Also, under the domestic law of the member, courts and other organs of that member may rely in the first instance on the official translation published in the Gazette. If, however, the official translation conflicts with the original English version, the member is obliged, under general principles of international law, to comply with the English rather than with a divergent foreign-language version of the Agreement.

## 2. ORDINARY OR TECHNICAL MEANING OF WORDS AND PHRASES

Generally, a treaty shall be interpreted in good faith "with the ordinary meaning to be given to the terms of the treaty."[5] There are, of course, numerous provisions throughout the Fund Agreement

---

[4] For original members, this obligation is set forth in Art. XX, Sec. 2(a). For other than original members, this obligation is prescribed in the respective paragraph of the Membership Resolution. See paragraph 8(b) of Resolution No. 21-8 of the Board of Governors of the Fund (Membership for Guyana) in IMF, *Summary Proceedings*, 1966, p. 246.

[5] See the Draft Articles on the Law of Treaties, adopted by the International Law Commission of the United Nations at its 893rd Session on July 18, 1966. U.N. General Assembly, 21st Sess. *Official Records*, Supp. 9 (A/6309/Rev.1), Art. 27(1). The Draft Articles, together with the Commentary of the Commission, have also been published in *American Journal of International Law*, vol. 61 (January 1967) pp. 263-463. See, however, Art. 27(4) of the Draft Articles, which reads: "A special meaning shall be given to a term if it is established that the parties so intended."

which are readily understandable or which may be interpreted in terms of the "ordinary meaning" of the words or phrases employed. At the same time, the Fund Agreement, as the organic law of an international institution "which provides machinery for consultation and collaboration on international monetary problems," abounds with terms that are meaningful only as technical terms. To these terms the principle that treaty terms are to be interpreted by reference to their ordinary meaning cannot apply.[6]

Among the technical terms that are used in the Fund Agreement three different categories may be distinguished: (1) technical terms that have a special meaning for technicians—for example, "spot-exchange transactions" [Article IV, Section 3(i)]; (2) technical terms which, though frequently used by technicians, have a special meaning in the context of the Fund Agreement—for example, the definition of a member's holdings of convertible currencies as the "holdings of the currencies of other members which are not availing themselves of the transitional arrangements under Article XIV, Section 2" [Article XIX(d)]; and (3) terms that purport to have a technical meaning in the context of the Fund Agreement, but which are not defined in the Fund Agreement and which never have been conclusively interpreted by the Fund—for example, the term "fundamental disequilibrium" in Article IV, Section 5(a).[7]

In addition to the foregoing categories of terms, the Fund has introduced technical terms such as "gold tranche," "credit tranche," or "stand-by arrangements." These terms, used time and again in official documents of the Fund, are understandable only by reference

---

[6] See, on this point, also V. D. Degan, *L'Interprétation des Accords en Droit International* (The Hague: Nijhoff, 1963), p. 89; "Malgré sa vaste application par la jurisprudence internationale, la règle du sens ordinaire est limitée par sa contre-règle, celle du sens technique."

[7] On September 26, 1946, the Executive Directors of the Fund rendered an interpretation under Art. XVIII(a) of the Fund Agreement relating to steps to correct a fundamental disequilibrium. The operative paragraph of this decision (No. 71-2) reads as follows: "The Executive Directors interpret the Articles of Agreement to mean that steps which are necessary to protect a member from unemployment of a chronic or persistent character, arising from pressure on its balance of payments, are among the measures necessary to correct a fundamental disequilibrium; and that in each instance in which a member proposes a change in the par value of its currency to correct a fundamental disequilibrium the Fund will be required to determine, in the light of all relevant circumstances, whether in its opinion the proposed change is necessary to correct the fundamental disequilibrium." It should be clear that this interpretation does not purport to furnish a generally applicable definition of "fundamental disequilibrium."

to the Fund Agreement as interpreted through the years by the Fund. The implications of these terms will be discussed below, in Part III of this study, in connection with the principal types of Fund operations.

In brief, it is not always easy to determine whether ordinary or technical language is used. Moreover, where technical language is used, it is frequently difficult to pinpoint the exact meaning of technical terms employed in Fund parlance.

### 3. CONTINGENT PROVISIONS

There are numerous contingent provisions in the Fund Agreement, that is to say, provisions dependent on future contingencies for which no date could possibly be specified. To illustrate: (1) Under Article XX, Section 4(a) the Fund was to notify members of the date on which it expected shortly to be in a position to begin exchange transactions; in practice, the Fund designated September 12, 1946 as this date.[8] (2) The effectiveness of other contingent provisions, for example, those relating to original members, was dependent primarily on action taken by members not later than December 31, 1945.[9] (3) Other contingent provisions, for example, those relating to adjustment of quotas, require the initiative of the member requesting a quota adjustment as well as the concurrence of the members representing at least 80 per cent of the total voting power (Article III, Section 2).[10]

Up to now the Fund has not issued an annotated edition of the Fund Agreement that would permit the reader to determine whether, to what extent, and at which point in time, the numerous contingent provisions of the Fund Agreement became applicable or inapplicable. The present writer has endeavored to supply such information in the above-cited work entitled *The International Monetary Fund: Legal Bases, Structure, Functions*. The staff of the Fund has been engaged for quite some time in the preparation of a *Twenty Years History*. Pending the publication of this *History*, the *Annual Reports* of the Fund,[11] the 23 *Summary Proceedings* of the Annual Meetings of the

[8] For additional information on this point, see Hans Aufricht, *The International Monetary Fund: Legal Bases, Structure, Functions* (London and New York: F. A. Praeger, 1964), p. 9, fn. 4 (This source is hereafter cited as "Aufricht, *The International Monetary Fund*."

[9] See Art. II, Sec. 1 and Art. XX, Sec. 2(e).

[10] The proposed Amendment to the Articles of Agreement requires an 85 per cent majority for any decision on a general review of quotas, see below p. 66.

[11] The Fund's *Annual Reports* have been issued for the Fund's fiscal years

Board of Governors,[12] and the Fund's *Annual Reports on Exchange Restrictions*[13] are the most significant official sources of information on changes in the law and practice of the Fund.

## 4. SIGNIFICANCE OF FIGURES IN THE FUND AGREEMENT

Many of the figures included in the original Fund Agreement are by now obsolete. Under Article III, Section 1 of the Fund Agreement, the quotas of the original members of the Fund—that is, the members accepting the Agreement not later than December 31, 1945—were to be those set forth in Schedule A.[14] However, all figures contained therein, with the exception of the quota of China, have been superseded as a result of general and individual quota increases that have taken place between 1947 and 1968.[15] Also, the rates of charges provided for in Article V, Section 8(c) and (d) are no longer in force; they have been modified from time to time, in accordance with Article V, Section 8(e). The number of Executive Directors, originally limited to twelve—five appointed and seven elected—has been increased to 20, in accordance with the last sentence of Article XII, Section 3(b).[16]

The foregoing examples do not purport to constitute a complete enumeration of all relevant figures that appear in the Fund Agreement, but merely to point up the fact that even some of the basic numerical assumptions of the Agreement have been subject to change in the law and practice of the Fund in the period 1944-1968. Many factors account for these changes; but the most pervasive one is the expansion

---

1947 through 1968; in addition there is an *Annual Report* for 1946. The full title of the latest *Annual Report* is International Monetary Fund, *Annual Report of the Executive Directors for the Fiscal Year ended April 30, 1968.*

[12] The *Summary Proceedings* of the Annual Meetings of the Board of Governors, hereafter cited for example, "IMF, *Summary Proceedings, 1967*," cover the Annual Meetings from 1946 to 1968.

[13] From 1950 to 1968 the Fund has issued 19 *Annual Reports on Exchange Restrictions*, hereafter cited for example, "IMF, *Nineteenth Annual Report on Exchange Restrictions, 1968.*"

[14] For Schedule-A Quotas, see Appendix III.

[15] For synopsis of Quotas and Voting Powers in the Fund, as of November 1, 1968, see below Appendix II.

[16] For list of appointed and elected Executive Directors as of November 1, 1968, see Appendix II. It should also be noted that Schedule C of the Fund Agreement has been superseded by subsequent Rules, adopted by the Board of Governors, for the Conduct of the Regular Election of Executive Directors of the Fund. For text of the 1966 Election Rules, as approved by Board of Governors Resolution No. 21-7, see IMF, *Summary Proceedings, 1966*, pp. 223-229.

5

of Fund membership from 22 countries on December 27, 1945 to 111 members on November 1, 1968.[17]

## 5. ARE THE RIGHTS AND OBLIGATIONS OF MEMBERS UNIFORM?

Each government about to join the Fund is required to deposit with the Government of the United States of America an Instrument of Acceptance stating that it accepts the Fund Agreement "in accordance with its law and has taken all steps necessary to enable it to carry out all of its obligations under this Agreement" [Article XX, Section 2(a)]. Although there are many obligations that apply to all members,[18] there is a conspicuous lack of uniformity regarding specific obligations. The same holds true, *mutatis mutandis*, for the rights of members under the Fund Agreement. Some of the principal reasons for the lack of uniformity of members' obligations and rights may be briefly indicated:

### (a) *Original and Other Members*

Generally speaking, the provisions of the Fund Agreement are addressed to the original members. Members joining after December 31, 1946, pursuant to Article II, Section 2 of the Fund Agreement, are subject to the Articles of Agreement and the terms and conditions of the Resolutions of the Board of Governors of the Fund relating to the admission to membership of the country concerned (hereafter referred to as "Membership Resolution"). By contrast, no individual Membership Resolution was adopted for the ten members joining between January 1 and December 31, 1946[19] under Resolution No. IM-9 of the Board of Governors.[20] However this may be, in the period January 1, 1947 through September 30, 1968, 74 countries joined the Fund under individual Membership Resolutions.[21]

[17] The IMF, *International Financial Statistics*, issues monthly figures relating to the status, financial structure, and operations of the Fund. In general, however, no legal link is shown between the relevant provisions of the Fund Agreement and these figures.

[18] The IMF pamphlet edition of the Fund Agreement (cited in fn. 2, p. 1, above) contains a helpful guide to the principal provisions concerning "Obligations of members" on pages 61-62.

[19] For text of this Resolution, see IMF, *Selected Documents: Board of Governors Inaugural Meeting* (Savannah, Ga.: March 8 to 18, 1946), p. 21.

[20] For detailed information on the ten countries and the dates of acceptance of membership under Resolution No. IM-9 of the Board of Governors, see Aufricht, *The International Monetary Fund*, pp. 20-21.

[21] The texts of these Membership Resolutions have been published by the Fund in the *Summary Proceedings* of the Annual Meeting of the Board of Gov-

Generally, if a Membership Resolution contains provisions that differ from what the Fund Agreement provides for original members—for example, the provisions governing the determination of the initial par value—the relevant provisions of the Membership Resolution rather than those of the Fund Agreement apply.

## (b) Article-XIV Members and Article-VIII Members

In Fund practice a distinction is frequently made between Article XIV-members and Article-VIII members; the former category of members comprises those that have availed themselves of the transitional arrangements of Article XIV, Section 2, and notified the Fund of their intention to do so under the authority of Article XIV, Section 3.[22]

Article-XIV members are exempt from certain obligations provided for in Article VIII, Sections 2 and 3—that is, from the obligation to seek the approval of the Fund in respect of certain exchange restrictions, multiple-currency practices, or discriminatory currency arrangements—and from the obligation of Article VIII, Section 4, to convert certain foreign-held balances. Article XIV, Section 2 expressly empowers members to maintain and adapt to changing circumstances the restrictions on payments and transfers in respect of current transactions that were in effect at the time the member joined the Fund.[23] Beginning with March 1, 1952, reliance on the transitional arrangements obligates members to consult annually with the Fund on the retention of those restrictions which, in the absence of Article XIV, Sec-

---

ernors of the year in which they were adopted (that is, if the date of adoption is not later than the day of the termination of the respective Annual Meeting). For a discussion of the principal features of Membership Resolutions, see Aufricht, *The International Monetary Fund*, pp. 22-23.

[22] It may be inferred from the wording of Art. XIV, Sec. 3 that the authorization of members to avail themselves of the transitional arrangements of Art. XIV, Sec. 2, and thus to become an Article-XIV member, was to be reserved for original members; in Fund practice the authorization has also been extended to other than original members.

[23] Under Art. XIV, Sec. 2 of the Fund Agreement "members whose territories have been occupied by the enemy" are expressly empowered to "introduce where necessary" restrictions on payments and transfers in respect of current international transactions. As far as can be ascertained, no member of the Fund has ever introduced exchange restrictions on current transactions by virtue of this provision. It appears that this provision, which forms part of the transitional arrangements of Art. XIV, Sec. 2, is now deemed by the Fund as no longer applicable; see for example, IMF, *Eighteenth Annual Report on Exchange Restrictions* (Washington: 1967), p. 2.

tion 2, would require approval of the Fund under Article VIII, Section 2 or 3.[24]

An Article-VIII member—that is a member not availing itself of the transitional arrangements of Article XIV, Section 2—may not, without the approval of the Fund,[25] impose restrictions on payments or transfers in respect of current international transactions [Article VIII, Section 2(a)], or prescribe or permit "multiple-currency practices," or discriminatory currency arrangements (Article VIII, Section 3).[26] An Article-VIII member is obligated to purchase certain foreign-held balances in accordance with the provisions of Article VIII, Section 4. Moreover, under the decision of June 1, 1960, of the Executive Board of the Fund, members in Article-VIII status[27] are also expected to consult periodically with the Fund at intervals of about one year.[28]

(c) *The Fund's Authority to Approve Exemptions from Specified Obligations*

Differences in the obligations of members under the Fund Agreement may also be the result of the Fund's exercise of its authority to approve specified measures by members which, in the absence of such affirmative action, would constitute a breach of the member's obligations—for example, of the obligations provided for in Article VIII, Section 2(a). Actually, there are Article-VIII members which, as prescribed in Article VIII, Section 2(a), do not impose restrictions

[24] On the point that the currencies of Article-XIV members are not considered as "convertible currencies" in the sense of Art. XIX(d), see above p. 3.

[25] However, even an Article-VIII member is authorized under Art. VII, Sec. 3(b), after consultation with the Fund, to impose temporary limitations on the freedom of exchange operations in a currency that has formally been declared by the Fund to be "scarce currency" under Art. VII, Sec. 3(a). Up to September 30, 1968, the Fund has never formally declared the currency of any member to be a "scarce currency" under Art. VII, Sec. 3(a).

[26] For purposes of this study the terms "multiple-currency practices" and "multiple exchange rates" are deemed interchangeable. On the implications of these terms and on the "single-rate" concept of the Fund Agreement, see Hans Aufricht, "The Fund Agreement and the Legal Theory of Money," *Oesterreichische Zeitschrift fuer Oeffentliches Recht*, vol. X(1959), pp. 37-38 and 40-41.

[27] See paragraph 3 of the June 1 decision of the Executive Directors in IMF, *Annual Report, 1960*, p. 30.

[28] As of April 30, 1968, the following 31 members of the Fund had accepted Article-VIII status: Australia, Austria, Belgium, Bolivia, Canada, Costa Rica, Denmark, Dominican Republic, El Salvador, France, Germany, Guatemala, Guyana, Haiti, Honduras, Ireland, Italy, Jamaica, Japan, Kuwait, Luxembourg, Mexico, Netherlands, Nicaragua, Norway, Panama, Peru, Saudi Arabia, Sweden, United Kingdom, United States.

on payments and transfers in respect of current international transactions, while other Article-VIII members impose such restrictions, with the Fund's approval.

## (d) *Special Rights of Members*

While the voting procedures of most international organizations—for example, the United Nations—confer upon each member one vote, the weighted-voting regime of the Fund is a built-in exception to the equality of member countries in the Fund.[29] Under Article XII, Section 5(a) of the Fund Agreement, "Each member shall have two hundred fifty votes plus one additional vote for each part of the quota equivalent to one hundred thousand United States dollars." Thus on November 1, 1968 the United States—the member with the largest quota—had 51,850 votes, or 21.63 per cent of the total voting power of the 111 members of the Fund. By contrast, Botswana had 280 votes, or 0.12 per cent of the total voting power.

Although the provisions of the Fund Agreement on weighted voting are of special interest to students and functionaries of international organizations, the significance of these provisions in the day-to-day decisions of the Fund should not be overestimated. In most instances, the decisions of the Executive Board and of the Board of Governors are taken without any formal or roll-call vote. In the Executive Board, the Managing Director (or the officer acting as Chairman in the absence of the Managing Director) "will ordinarily ascertain the sense of the meeting in lieu of a formal vote."[30] In the Board of Governors, the Chairman may ascertain the sense of the meeting in lieu of a formal vote but he shall require a formal vote upon the request of any Governor.[31]

Two examples may suffice to illustrate special rights accorded to the United States and the United Kingdom as a result of their large quota and voting rights: (1) The original Articles of Agreement provide that a "four-fifths majority of the total voting power shall be required for any change in quota" (Article III, Section 2); it thereby gives the United States a veto power over a proposed change in the

[29] For status of quotas and voting power in the Fund, as of November 1, 1968, see Appendix II.
[30] See Rule C-10 of the Rules and Regulations of the Fund. Under this provision, however, any Executive Director may require a formal vote to be taken, with votes cast as prescribed in Art. XII, Sec. 3(i).
[31] See Sec. 11 of the By-Laws of the Fund.

quota of any other members so long as the voting power of the United States exceeds 20 per cent of the total voting power.[32] (2) The United States and the United Kingdom, acting jointly or separately, can veto any comprehensive change of the price of monetary gold by means of a so-called uniform change in par values under Article IV, Section 7, since only the voting powers of the United States and the United Kingdom exceed 10 per cent of the total votes. The relevant clause of this section declares such changes permissible with the concurrence of "a majority of the total voting power . . . provided each such change is approved by every member which has ten per cent or more of the total of the quotas."[33]

[32] Under the proposed Amendment of the Articles of Agreement an 85 per cent majority of the total voting power is required for a general review of quotas; see below p. 66. On the implications of the 85 per cent vote, see Fritz Machlup, *Remaking the International Monetary System: The Rio Agreement and Beyond* (Baltimore: Johns Hopkins Press, 1968) p. 41. It should be noted that the relative voting strength of the United States decreased from 37.90 per cent on December 27, 1945 to 22.12 per cent on November 1, 1968. On "weighted voting" in the Fund, see Aufricht, *The International Monetary Fund*, pp. 41-43.

[33] Under the proposed Amendment of the Articles of Agreement an 85 per cent majority of the total voting power is required for decisions on uniform proportionate changes in the par values of the currencies of all members; see below p. 66.

## II. INTERPRETATIONS OF THE FUND AGREEMENT

### 1. LEGAL TECHNIQUES OF INTERPRETATION

In a sense, any deliberate attempt to clarify the implications of the rules set forth in the Fund Agreement may be considered an interpretation. Thus we encounter "interpretations" of the Fund Agreement in numerous monographs, articles, and Parliamentary proceedings that are designed to explain the meaning of the Fund Agreement, or any of its provisions, as such or by reference to the probable economic effect of actions by members of the Fund or by the Fund itself. However, only a minimal segment of the vast literature on the Fund Agreement is concerned with the principal legal techniques of interpretation.[34] Considering the current plans for a formal amendment of the Fund Agreement, the legal aspects of interpreting the Fund Agreement, always of great though frequently neglected importance, have taken on added significance.

Among the various conceivable approaches to treaty interpretation, the so-called textual approach has now been formally endorsed by the International Law Commission of the United Nations on the ground that "the text must be presumed to be the authentic expression of the intention of the parties; and that in consequence, the starting point of interpretation is the elucidation of the meaning of the text, not an investigation *ab initio* into the intentions of the parties."[35]

It follows from the general rules of interpretation, underlying the textual approach, that the terms of the treaty shall, in principle, be interpreted by reference to their ordinary meaning, subject to the

[34] For a bibliographical survey of publications relating to the Fund, see Martin L. Loftus, "The International Monetary Fund, 1946-1950: A Selected Bibliography" in IMF, *Staff Papers*, vol. I (April 1951), pp. 471-491; vol. III (April 1953), pp. 171-180; vol. IV (August 1955), pp. 467-481; vol. VI (November 1958), pp. 476-496; vol. IX (November 1962), pp. 449-489; vol. XII (November 1965), pp. 470-524, and vol. XV (March 1968), pp. 143-195.

[35] The quoted passage is from the Commission's commentary to Art. 27 of the Draft Articles in *American Journal of International Law*, vol. 61 (January 1967), p. 354. In favor of the textual approach, see also the 1956 Resolution of the Institute of International Law, Art. 1(1), which reads: "L'accord des parties s'étant réalisé sur le texte du traité, il y a lieu de prendre le sens naturel et ordinaire des termes de ce texte comme base d'interprétation. Les termes des dispositions du traité doivent être interprétés dans le contexte entier, selon la bonne foi et à la lumière des principes du droit international." *Annuaire de l'Institut de Droit International*, vol. 46 (1956), p. 349.

proviso that a special or technical meaning shall be given to a term if an intention of the parties to this effect may be inferred from the wording of the treaty.[36] The terms of the treaty shall furthermore not be viewed in isolation, but "in their context and in the light of its object and purpose."[37]

Whenever the textual approach to treaty interpretation is applied, in the view of the International Law Commission the following considerations may also be taken into account: (1) any subsequent agreement between the parties regarding the interpretation of the treaty; (2) any subsequent practice in the application of the treaty which establishes the understanding of the parties regarding its interpretation; and (3) any relevant rules of international law applicable in the relations between the parties.[38] If the textual approach leaves the meaning of the terms to be interpreted ambiguous or obscure, or leads to a result that is manifestly absurd or unreasonable, recourse may be had to supplementary means of interpretation, including reference to the preparatory work of the treaty and the circumstances of its conclusion.[39]

The foregoing principal rules governing the interpretation of treaties as formulated by the International Law Commission are presumably not designed to preclude, where appropriate, recourse to widely recognized maxims of interpretation. These include the following: (1) a rule of a higher level prevails over a rule of a lower level; (2) a special rule prevails over a general rule; and (3) a later rule prevails over an earlier rule. Also, the judicious blending of these maxims of interpretation that is deemed permissible by jurists and by international and national tribunals should not be excluded from the admissible legal techniques of interpretation.[40]

## 2. PREPARATORY WORK

The preparatory work (*travaux préparatoires*) in the broader sense relating to the Fund Agreement comprises primarily the American

[36] See Art. 27(4) of the Draft Articles (quoted above in footnote 5) and commentary thereon in *American Journal of International Law*, vol. 61 (January 1967), p. 358.

[37] See Art. 27(1) of the Draft Articles, *ibid.*, p. 348; see also p. 355.

[38] See Art. 27(3) of the Draft Articles, *ibid.*, p. 348; see also pp. 356-358.

[39] See Art. 28 of the Draft Articles, *ibid.*, p. 349; see also pp. 358-361.

[40] See, on this point, Hans Aufricht, "Supersession of Treaties in International Law," *Cornell Law Quarterly* (Summer 1952), especially p. 700.

*Proposal for a United and Associated Nations Stabilization Fund* (the "White Plan"),[41] the British *Proposals for an International Clearing Union*,[42] the *Joint Statement by Experts on the Establishment of an International Monetary Fund*,[43] and the above mentioned *Bretton Woods Proceedings*.

(a) *The White Plan and the Keynes Plan*

The United States released its Proposal on April 7, 1943. It became known as the "White Plan," referring to Harry D. White, of the U.S. Treasury Department, who was credited with being principally responsible for its formulation.[44] The British Proposal, in turn, was released on April 8, 1943. Authorship of this Plan was ascribed to John Maynard Keynes and it, accordingly, came to be known as the Keynes Plan.[45] For more than a year prior to the release of the *Joint Statement of Experts* on April 21, 1944, the discussions of the monetary technicians inside and outside the governments of the United and Associated Nations centered on the Keynes and White Plans. A revised version of the latter had been released on July 10, 1943.[46] The concentration of the discussion on these plans is understandable in view of the economic importance of the United States and the United Kingdom, the prestige of the authors and their role as principal negotiators for the two countries in the period preceding the Bretton Woods Conference, and the need for surveying the similarities and differences of the two plans before a considered judgment on their relative merits could be formed. There can be no doubt that even today the comparative analyses of the two plans in the works of John

[41] For text of the original version of the White Plan, see *Proceedings and Documents of the United Nations Monetary and Financial Conference, Bretton Woods, New Hampshire, July 1 to 22, 1944* (Washington: 1948), vol. II, pp. 1536-1547. (This document is hereafter cited as *"Bretton Woods Proceedings."*)

[42] For text, see *Bretton Woods Proceedings*, vol. II, pp. 1548-1573.

[43] For text, see *Bretton Woods Proceedings*, vol. II, pp. 1629-1636. The complete heading of the Joint Statement reads: "Joint Statement by Experts on the Establishment of an International Monetary Fund of the United and Associated Nations."

[44] On Harry D. White, see Richard N. Gardner, *Sterling-Dollar Diplomacy* (Oxford: Clarendon Press, 1956), p. 73.

[45] For text of the Keynes Plan or the "Proposals for an International Clearing Union," see *Bretton Woods Proceedings*, vol. II, pp. 1548-1573.

[46] For text of the "Preliminary Draft Outline of a Proposal for an International Stabilization Fund of the United and Associated Nations," see *Bretton Woods Proceedings*, vol. II, pp. 1600-1615.

Parke Young,[47] George N. Halm,[48] and Richard N. Gardner,[49] and of their subsequent modifications at the Bretton Woods Conference constitute most valuable aids to a realistic appraisal of the Fund Agreement as it emerged. However, it should not be overlooked that the *Joint Statement of Experts* was the basic working document at the Bretton Woods Conference and that the *Joint Statement*, in turn, was substantially modified and amended in the course of the Conference.[50]

### (b) *Joint Statement and Bretton Woods Proceedings*

As previously stated, for purposes of legal interpretation of treaties recourse to preparatory work is admissible in certain situations.[51] However, recourse to preparatory work will yield persuasive conclusions only if the corresponding formulations of the preparatory work are clear, unequivocal, and do not lead to manifestly absurd or unreasonable results.

The *Bretton Woods Proceedings* have frequently been consulted in the day-to-day work of the Fund to confirm or clarify the meaning of individual provisions of the Fund Agreement as such, or in the context of the Agreement. While some have looked upon the material published in the *Proceedings* as being in the nature of *travaux préparatoires*, others, including a former General Counsel of the Fund, have expressed the view that such an evaluation is not justified.[52]

Although perusal of the *Joint Statement of Experts* and the *Bretton Woods Proceedings* may be informative and shed some light on the

[47] John Parke Young, "Developing Plans for an International Monetary Fund and a World Bank," *Department of State Bulletin*, vol. XXIII (November 13, 1950), pp. 778-790.

[48] George N. Halm, *International Monetary Cooperation* (Chapel Hill: University of North Carolina Press, 1945).

[49] Richard N. Gardner, *op.cit.*

[50] See, on this point, Robert Mossé, "Souvenirs de Bretton Woods," in *Le Monde* (September 26, 1967), p. 29: "On n'a jamais comparé systématiquement la déclaration commune (le Joint Statement pour les initiés) avec l'acte final, afin de mesurer l'apport propre de la conférence, c'est à dire, en somme, l'apport des pays autres que les Etats-Unis et la Grande-Bretagne." The author of this statement served at the Bretton Woods Conference as the Reporting Delegate of Committee 2 (Operations of the Fund) of Commission I.

[51] See Art. 28 of the Draft Articles, *American Journal of International Law*, vol. 61 (January 1967), p. 349; see also pp. 358-361.

[52] J.E.S. Fawcett, "The Place of Law in an International Organization," *British Yearbook of International Law*, vol. XXXVI (1960) p. 333, writes: "The Bretton Woods Conference kept no official or systematic records of its proceedings, though a number of preliminary drafts of provisions of the Agreement, reports of Conference committees, and summary notes of various debates and proceedings were assembled and published."

substance of the problem at issue, it is generally doubtful whether from a legal viewpoint recourse to these documents will yield more conclusive results than a conscientious and enlightened textual approach to treaty interpretation. There are, however, exceptions. In particular, there are terms or clauses in the Fund Agreement that are the result of compromise and therefore obscure, whereas an earlier drafting proposal would have been clearer in meaning.[53]

### 3. INTERPRETATION OF THE FUND AGREEMENT BY THE FUND

#### (a) Exclusive Jurisdiction of the Fund

Under the law and practice of the Fund the interpretation of the Fund Agreement is reserved exclusively to the Fund. The principle of exclusive jurisdiction in matters of interpretation has been expressed as follows in Article XVIII(a); "Any question of interpretation of the provisions of this Agreement arising between any member and the Fund or between any members of the Fund shall be submitted to the Executive Directors for their decision." The decision of the Executive Directors is final, unless a member demands that it be reviewed by the Board of Governors. In the period 1946 to 1961, the Executive Directors rendered and published at least eight interpretations under Article XVIII(a).[54] No member invoked Article XVIII(b)

[53] For example, the "unenforceability clause" of Art. VIII, Sec. 2(b) centers on "exchange contracts," while earlier proposals (see *Bretton Woods Proceedings*, Document 32, vol. I, pp. 54-55 and Document 236, vol. I, p. 334) use the term "exchange transactions." Considering that the term "exchange contracts" has neither a generally accepted technical meaning nor an ordinary meaning, it would appear preferable, for purposes of interpretation, to replace the term "exchange contracts" by the term "exchange transactions." The unenforceability clause would thus read as follows: "Exchange transactions which involve the currency of any member and which are contrary to the exchange control regulations of that member maintained or imposed consistently with this Agreement shall be unenforceable in the territories of any member."

[54] See Aufricht, *The International Monetary Fund*, p. 13. Hexner and Fawcett refer to nine such decisions, since they are of the opinion that Executive Board decision No. 541 (56/39) of July 25, 1956 relating to controls of capital transfers has also been taken pursuant to Art. XVIII(a). See, on this point, Ervin P. Hexner, "Interpretation by Public International Organizations of their Basic Instruments," *American Journal of International Law*, vol. 53 (1959), pp. 357-358, fn. 31. The IMF publication *Selected Decisions of Executive Directors*, Third Issue (Washington: January 1965), lists on p. XII nine such decisions, by including Executive Board decisions No. 905 (59/32) and No. 1272 (61/53) relating to the Fund's Investment Program as interpretations under Art. XVIII(a). These latter decisions are, in effect, modifications of the basic decision No. 488-(56/5) of January 25, 1956 on Investment of Fund's Assets.

to have a question of interpretation referred to the Board of Governors.

Actually, formal interpretations under Article XVIII are not the only kind of interpretation in Fund practice. In addition, there are decisions of the Executive Directors, rendered in writing, which interpret individual provisions of the Fund Agreement but were not reached by virtue of Article XVIII.[55] Also, the staff renders legal opinions on many questions arising under the Fund Agreement. Finally, interpretations may be implicit in the practical construction of the Agreement, particularly in the By-Laws and Rules and Regulations of the Fund,[56] as well as in the decisions and resolutions of the Executive Directors and the Board of Governors.

## (b) Interpretative Decisions of the Executive Board

Although the interpretations of the Fund Agreement by means of Executive Board decision are presumably conclusive, it has been recognized that such interpretations may, in turn, be subject to interpretation[57] and/or that they may be supplemented by subsequent Executive Board decisions. Moreover, it is reasonable to assume that the maxim that the later rule prevails over the earlier rule applies also to interpretative decisions of the Executive Board, in the sense that a later decision on the same subject matter supersedes an earlier decision thereon.

For example, the Executive Board's decision No. 71-2 of September 26, 1946, provides "that authority to use the resources of the Fund is limited to use in accordance with its purposes to give temporary assistance in financing balance of payments deficits on current account for monetary stabilization operations."[58] This decision has been supplemented, "by way of clarification," as not precluding "the use of the Fund's resources for capital transfers in accordance with the provisions of the Articles, including Article VI."[59]

[55] In this category are the majority of the decisions of the Executive Directors published by the Fund in IMF, *Selected Decisions*, cited above in footnote 54.

[56] IMF, *By-Laws: Rules and Regulations*, 26th Issue, August 10, 1966.

[57] See, for example, Joseph Gold, *The Fund Agreement in the Courts* (Washington: 1962), p. 108, who, in commenting on Executive Board decision No. 446-4 of June 10, 1949 relating to the unenforceability of exchange contracts, states: "The Fund's interpretation was not intended to be, and quite obviously is not, an interpretation of all aspects of the provision."

[58] For the text of the decision see IMF, *Selected Decisions*, p. 54.

[59] For text of the supplementing decision No. 1238-(61/43) of July 28, 1961, see *ibid.*

There are other decisions of the Executive Board that are in the nature of amending decisions; for example, decision No. 2192-(66/81) of September 20, 1966, under the following heading: "Compensatory Financing of Export Fluctuations: Amendment of 1963 Decision."[60]

In addition to interpretative decisions of the Executive Board that expressly amend or supplement preceding decisions, there are others that repeal earlier decisions by implication. Several decisions of this kind have been included in the 1965 pamphlet edition of *Selected Decisions of the Executive Directors*. There is, however, no consolidated edition that expressly indicates whether and to what extent an earlier conflicting decision has been superseded by a later interpretative decision. In connection with the formal amendment of the Fund Agreement, proposed in the Report of April 1968,[61] it would appear advisable that the Fund take an inventory of the interpretative decisions extant, consolidate and harmonize those that supplement or amend one another, and weed out decisions that are no longer valid.

[60] For text of the amending decision, see IMF, *Annual Report, 1967*, pp. 159-161; for text of the initial decision on the subject No. 1477-(63/8) of February 27, 1963, see IMF, *Annual Report*, 1963, pp. 196-199 and IMF, *Selected Decisions*, pp. 40-43.

[61] Cited above, fn. 3.

## III. THE DRAWING RIGHTS OF MEMBERS—LAW
## AND POLICY

### 1. AUTOMATIC OR CONDITIONAL DRAWING RIGHTS
### (SEPTEMBER 1943-JULY 1944)

The discussions between British and American representatives that were carried on in Washington in September 1943 revealed a fundamental difference of approach to the nature and operations of the proposed Fund. As reported by John Parke Young, "The British believed that the Fund should operate as an automatic institution with a minimum of discretion on the part of its management, whereas the United States believed that the Fund could be most effective in achieving its purpose if its operations were conducted on a discretionary basis."[62]

The determination on the part of the British representatives to limit the Fund's discretion in granting or refusing requests by members for purchases of currencies of other members is clearly reflected in a letter of October 17, 1943, from Keynes to Viner, in which Keynes formulated his preference for automatic access to the Fund's resources as follows: "Our view has been very strongly that if countries are to be given sufficient confidence they must be able to rely in all normal circumstances on drawing a substantial part of their quota without policing or facing unforeseen obstacles."[63] It is conspicuous that this statement recognizes only one limiting condition, namely, the size of the member's quota as it refers to the ability of "drawing a substantial part" of that quota. Otherwise, there is no reference to the purposes or provisions of the proposed Fund, nor to the decision-making powers of its organs, except in a negative way, since the Fund shall refrain from "policing" the exercise of the drawing rights of members. In addition, the assertion that the member shall be entitled in normal circumstances to draw on the Fund reflects an amazing indifference to one of the basic assumptions of the White plan, namely, that the Fund may, in principle, sell the currencies of mem-

[62] John Parke Young, "Developing Plans for an International Monetary Fund and a World Bank," *Department of State Bulletin*, vol. XXIII (November 13, 1950), p. 783.

[63] The above passage is quoted from Richard N. Gardner, *Sterling-Dollar Diplomacy* (Oxford: Clarendon Press, 1956), p. 113.

bers which it holds to the monetary authorities of another member only if the "foreign exchange demanded from the Fund is required to meet an adverse balance of payments predominantly on current account with any member country."[64]

Considering that Keynes refers to drawings "in normal circumstances," it may be argued that the statement is compatible with the substance of clause V-2-a of the White plan only on the premise that an adverse balance of payments, predominantly on current account, is deemed to be a normal circumstance in which members of the Fund are expected to find themselves.

However this may be, the question arises whether the provisions of the Fund Agreement constitute a compromise between the opposing views on automatic versus conditional access to the Fund's resources, or whether the Fund Agreement, is to be interpreted as *not* containing any provisions that warrant automatic drawing rights. The former view is apparently favored by John Parke Young, who states: "The articles of agreement as finally adopted represented somewhat of a compromise of these views," that is, between the "automatic" and "discretionary" access to the Fund's resources.[65] Also, Richard N. Gardner writes: "The compromise finally worked out on this issue was embodied in the Articles of Agreement adopted at the Bretton Woods Conference."[66] But he adds the following words of caution: "One could not be sure from the wording of the Articles themselves whether the British or the American view on the subject would finally prevail."[67]

By contrast, arguments will be advanced presently to show that neither the White Plan nor the Fund Agreement has embodied the principle of unconditional drawing rights of members.

## 2. Drawing Rights under the Fund Agreement

The conditions governing the use of the Fund's resources by members, that is, their drawing rights, may be grouped under the follow-

---

[64] *Bretton Woods Proceedings*, vol. II, pp. 1605-1606.

[65] John Parke Young, *op.cit.*, p. 787.

[66] Richard N. Gardner, *op.cit.*, p. 113. See also the discussion of the compromise as reflected in the Joint Statement, chapter iii, 2(a)—a provision which corresponds to Art. V, Sec. 3(a) of the Fund Agreement—in Shigeo Horie, *The International Monetary Fund* (London: St. Martin's Press, 1964), p. 80. Horie observes on p. 81: "Regarding drawings on the Fund, whether limited or not, the regulations are not as clear as might be desirable."

[67] Richard N. Gardner, *op.cit.*, p. 114.

ing headings: (a) limitations of drawing rights of individual members, other than ineligibility to use the Fund's resources, (b) ineligibility to use the Fund's resources, and (c) limitations of the Fund's obligation to sell to a member the currency of another member.

## (a) *Limitations of Drawing Rights of Individual Members, Other than Ineligibility to Use the Fund's Resources*

Under Article V, Section 3(a)(iii), the maximum drawing rights of a member eligible to use the Fund's resources equal—in the absence of a waiver of conditions under Article V, Section 4—the member's gold subscription plus its quota. However, during any period of twelve months a member's maximum drawing right under this provision is generally limited to amounts not exceeding 25 per cent of its quota.

To illustrate: a member with a quota of $100 million, 25 per cent of which has been paid in gold, may draw up to $25 million in any period of twelve months and up to $125 million in five successive periods. This example assumes that at the date of the drawing the Fund's holdings of the member's currency have not been reduced through purchase by other members. If, however, at the date of the member's drawing the Fund's holdings of the member's currency have been reduced below 75 per cent of its quota, say, to 30 per cent of its quota, the limitation that a member may not draw more than one-fourth of its quota during any twelve-month period does not apply. In this instance, the member may draw up to 70 per cent (25 per cent plus 45 per cent) of its quota during such period.

Also, a member whose quota is, for example, $100 million and whose gold subscription equals only 10 per cent of its quota may have maximum drawing rights under Article V, Section 3(a)(iii) in excess of $110 million, even though the Fund's holdings of that member's currency have not been reduced through purchases by other members. If, for example, the Fund's holdings of the currency of member A have been reduced from 90 per cent of its quota to 75 per cent as a result of "repurchases" of its currency by A, A's maximum drawing rights under Article V, Section 3(a)(iii) will equal $125 million, notwithstanding the fact that, as assumed in the above example, A's initial gold subscription equals only 10 per cent of its quota.[68]

[68] The above example is designed to illustrate a situation where a member has incurred a "repurchase" obligation at the end of a financial year even though

20

As a matter of law, any drawing, during any twelve-month period, that would increase the Fund's holdings of the member's currency by more than 25 per cent of its quota (except where the Fund's holdings of that currency are less than 75 per cent of the member's quota) requires a special arrangement (waiver of conditions) between the member and the Fund, under Article V, Section 4. This provides that the Fund "may in its discretion, and on terms which safeguard its interests, waive any of the conditions prescribed" in Article V, Section 3(a). The first waiver of this kind was granted in August 1953, and such waivers have since been granted frequently.

Apart from the above quantitative limitations, the member's drawing rights may be exercised under Article V, Section 3(a)(i) only if the member represents that the currency which it desires to purchase from the Fund is presently needed for making in that currency payments[69] which are consistent with the provisions of the Fund Agreement.[70] This may refer, for example, to the provisions of Article VI, Section 1, which proscribes net use of the Fund's resources to meet a large or sustained outflow of capital,[71] or those of Article XIV, Section 1,

it has not engaged in an exchange transaction with the Fund during that year, possibly because the member's monetary reserves increased during the year.

[69] It appears that in Fund practice the clause relating to the "making in that currency payments" is no longer literally applied. Especially since the adoption of the Executive Board decision of July 20, 1962 on "Currencies to be Drawn and to be Used in Repurchases" (for text see IMF, *Selected Decisions*, pp. 33-39), a member desiring to make a purchase of currency or currencies from the Fund is expected to consult the Managing Director of the Fund about the currencies to be drawn. In determining the particular currency or currencies to be drawn, the Managing Director will take into consideration the balance of payments and the reserve position of the countries whose currencies are considered for drawings as well as the Fund's holdings of these currencies (IMF, *Selected Decisions*, pp. 36-37). In repurchases the Fund will accept any currency that is formally convertible under Art. VIII and of which the Fund's holdings are below 75 per cent of the quota, provided that the repurchasing member has consulted the Managing Director on the currencies to be used (IMF, *Selected Decisions*, p. 38).

[70] By decision No. 284-4 of March 10, 1948 (*Selected Decisions*, p. 19), the Executive Directors of the Fund have interpreted Art. V, Sec. 3(a)(i) by saying, in effect, that the Fund will normally not challenge the representation of the member referred to in that provision; nevertheless, the Fund may, for good reasons, challenge the correctness of this declaration as not in conformity with the provisions of the Fund Agreement. If the Fund concludes that a particular declaration is not correct "the Fund may postpone [the exchange transaction requested], or reject the request, or accept it subject to conditions." Up to November 1, 1968, the Fund has never invoked this right of challenging a representation of a member under Art. V, Sec. 3(a)(i).

[71] Under the proposed Amendment of Art. VI, Sec. 2 of the Fund Agreement a member shall be entitled to make gold-tranche purchases to meet capital transfers; see below p. 67.

which states that the Fund "is not intended to provide facilities for relief or reconstruction or to deal with international indebtedness" arising out of World War II.

Another condition that may preclude automatic access to the Fund's resources has been incorporated in Article XX, Section 4(i), which expressly empowers the Fund to postpone exchange transactions with any member if, in the opinion of the Fund, the transaction would lead to use of the resources of the Fund in a manner contrary to the purposes of the Fund Agreement or prejudicial to the Fund or its members.[72]

All of the above-mentioned conditions governing the use of the Fund's resources by members are, strictly speaking, prerequisites of a member's exchange transactions with the Fund. There is, however, one provision which is applicable only after a member has purchased currency from the Fund and only if the Fund finds, under Article V, Section 5, that that member "is using the resources of the Fund in a manner contrary to the purposes of the Fund." Under the special procedure prescribed in the provision, the Fund may limit the use of its resources by the member and may even declare the member ineligible to use the resources of the Fund.

(b) *Ineligibility to Use the Fund's Resources*

A member is precluded from having access to Fund resources if the Fund has previously declared the member to be ineligible to use the Fund's resources [Article V, Section 3(a)(iv)].

The Fund may, after having given the member due notice, declare a member ineligible to use the Fund's resources if any of the following contingencies obtains: (1) the member is using the resources of the Fund in a manner contrary to the purposes of the Fund (Article V, Section 5), (2) the member fails to comply with a request of the Fund to exercise appropriate controls to prevent a large or sustained outflow of capital (Article VI, Section 1), (3) the member persists in

[72] The Executive Directors, by decision No. 284-2 of March 10, 1948 (*Selected Decisions*, p. 106) have interpreted Art. XX, Sec. 4(i) as applicable only "in the case of a member which has had no previous exchange transaction with the Fund." In other words, the Fund's authority to postpone an exchange transaction under Art. XX, Sec. 4(i) is deemed to be limited to the first exchange transaction between a member and the Fund, and may not be exercised in respect of subsequent exchange transactions. Up to November 1, 1968 the Fund has never exercised the right of postponing an exchange transaction by express reference to Executive Board decision No. 284-2; this decision is not, however, an interpretation of the Fund Agreement under Art. XVIII(a).

22

maintaining restrictions that are inconsistent with the purposes of the Fund (Article XIV, Section 4), (4) the member fails to fulfil any of its obligations under the Fund Agreement [Article XV, Section 2(a)].

Moreover, under Article IV, Section 6, a member "shall be ineligible to use the resources of the Fund unless the Fund otherwise determines," if that member changes the par value of its currency despite the objection of the Fund, in cases where the Fund is entitled to object.[73]

(c) *Limitations of the Fund's Authority to Sell to a Member the Currency of Another Member*

Subject to the provisions of Article VII, Section 3 (relating to scarce currencies) and of Article XVI (emergency provisions), the Fund shall generally supply "a member, on the initiative of such member, with the currency of another member in exchange for gold or for the currency of the member desiring to make the purchase" (Article V, Section 2).

No member may purchase from the Fund a currency which the Fund has formally declared to be "scarce currency," under Article VII, Section 3. Under this provision, the Fund shall declare a currency to be scarce if demand for it seriously threatens the Fund's ability to supply that currency.[74] Up to November 1, 1968, the Fund has never formally declared the currency of any member to be a "scarce currency" under Article VII, Section 3.

To forestall the formal declaration of a currency as "scarce," the Fund may replenish its holdings of any member's currency by requiring the member to sell its currency to the Fund for gold [Article VII, Section 2(ii)]. By contrast, a special agreement between the member and the Fund has to be reached, whenever the Fund wishes to *borrow*

[73] By virtue of this provision, France became ineligible to use the Fund's resources as of January 25, 1948 (see IMF, *Annual Report, 1948*, p. 36 and pp. 76-78). In September 1949, following the devaluation of sterling, France consulted with the Fund on a proposal to unify her exchange system on the basis of the free-market dollar rate. "The French Government did not feel, however, that it was possible to declare a new par value for the franc. The Fund welcomed the modifications proposed by the French Government, considering them a measure of unification of the French exchange system." (The foregoing quotation is from IMF, *Annual Report, 1950*, p. 37.) On October 15, 1954, the Executive Board restored France's eligibility to use the Fund's resources (IMF, *Annual Report, 1955*, p. 88). France agreed with the Fund on a new par value, to take effect on December 29, 1958.

[74] Art. VII distinguishes between "scarcity of the Fund's holdings" (Art. VII, Sec. 3) of a particular currency and the "general scarcity of currency" (Art. VII, Sec. 1), that is, "a general scarcity of a particular currency."

the currency directly from the member or seeks to *borrow* the currency from some other source either within or outside the territories of the member concerned [Article VII, Section 2(i)].[75]

Under the emergency provisions of the Fund Agreement, the Executive Directors may, by unanimous vote, suspend for a period of not more than 120 days the operation (*inter alia*) of Article V, Section 3. Consequently, the Fund is precluded from selling the currency of any member during a period of 120 days following the decision of the Executive Directors to suspend temporarily the provisions enumerated in Article XVI, Section 1(a). Such a temporary suspension of the Fund's operations may be extended for an additional period of not more than 240 days, by a vote of four-fifths of the Board of Governors [Article XVI, Section 1(c)].

### 3. The Fund's Lending Policies

The legal right of a member to purchase from the Fund the currency of another member has been designated above as "drawing right." The term "lending policy" or "lending policies"[76] will be used in this study to refer to major policy pronouncements, whether or not issued in the form of decisions by the Executive Board, which the Fund has released over the years to clarify for members the scope of their drawing rights.

A historical survey reveals that in the period 1948-1952 the Fund formulated statements on its lending policies imposing on the use of its resources more stringent conditions than those provided in the Fund Agreement. Beginning with 1952, however, the Fund proclaimed on various occasions statements on its lending policies intended to assure members virtually automatic access to the Fund's resources—though even in these instances the Fund set forth specified limits.

(a) *1948-1952*

On April 5, 1948, the Fund's Executive Board adopted a decision[77] on the effect of the European Recovery Program (ERP) on the use

---

[75] In 1966 the Fund borrowed the equivalent of $250 million in Italian lire under this provision. (See IMF, *Annual Report, 1967*, p. 17 and p. 48, and IMF, *International Financial News Survey*, August 19, 1966, p. 269.)

[76] The term "lending policy" is used *inter alia* in Richard N. Gardner, *op.cit.*, p. 297. For comments on the Fund's lending policy in the period 1949-1953, see generally *Survey of United States International Finance*, published annually by the International Finance Section, Princeton University (1950-1954).

[77] The text of the Fund's Press Release of April 20, 1948, which incorporates the Executive Board decision of April 5, 1948 has been reproduced in IMF, *Annual Report, 1948*, pp. 74-75.

of the Fund's resources by those members who participated in the ERP. The key sentence of the decision reads: "For the first year [of the ERP] the attitude of the Fund and ERP should be that such members should request purchase of United States dollars from the Fund only in exceptional or unforeseen cases."[78] This decision remained substantially in effect in subsequent years. It was never formally repealed, but lapsed presumably simultaneously with the termination of the European Recovery Program.[79] So long as the ERP decision was in force, however, members of the Fund participating in the European Recovery Program were generally precluded from drawing dollars from the Fund. The Fund's lending policy, as reflected in the decision, was no doubt warranted in the circumstances of the times.

Detailed scrutiny of the question of whether other decisions of the Executive Board adopted in the period prior to 1952 also imposed conditions on the use of the Fund's resources over and above the conditions provided in the Fund Agreement is outside the scope of this study. Richard N. Gardner, for example, considers a decision which the Executive Board adopted to clarify the meaning of Article V, Section 3(a)(i) and has not repealed up to now as having the effect of deferring exchange transactions with members.[80]

(b) *The Decision of February 13, 1952*

The IMF *Annual Report, 1952* referred to the decision of February 13, 1952 by the Executive Board as "the most important step taken during the year in the evolution of policy" with respect to the use of the

[78] *Ibid.*, p. 74.

[79] It appears that the European Recovery Program came to an end by June 30, 1952 (see 82d Congress, 2d Session, House Document No. 523, Washington, 1952, *Report of Activities of the National Advisory Council on International Monetary and Financial Problems*, p. 12).

[80] See Richard N. Gardner, *op.cit.*, pp. 296-297: "In an important interpretation of their powers in June 1947 the Executive Directors declared that they could look behind the representations made by applicants for assistance and could determine whether in fact the applicants needed loans for the purposes stipulated in the Fund Articles. To put it bluntly, the Fund was not going to grant assistance to members unless it was assured that the aid would be used for short-term stabilization purposes and not for purposes of reconstruction. Since few members could give such assurances in the first half of 1947, the Fund engaged in virtually no exchange operations." The IMF, *Annual Report, 1947*, covering the fiscal year ending June 30, 1947, p. 31, reproduces principal features of the decision to which Gardner refers. In the IMF *Selected Decisions* a substantially identical interpretation is recorded on p. 19 as decision No. 284-4 of March 10, 1948. On the Fund's conservative lending policy in 1947-1948, see also Gardner, *op.cit.*, pp. 297-298.

Fund's resources by members.[81] The decision constituted indeed a new departure in that it generally was designed to encourage rather than discourage exchange transactions between members and the Fund.[82]

(i) *Quota drawings.* Paragraph 3 of the decision provides: "Each member can count on receiving the overwhelming benefit of any doubt respecting drawings which would raise the Fund's holdings of its currency to not more than its quota." Subsequently such drawings were called "drawings within the 'gold tranche.' "[83] The legal significance of the formulation in paragraph 3 of the decision on the drawing rights of members is by no means clear. The draftsmen of this paragraph may have been inspired by the wording of Article XIV, Section 5 of the Fund Agreement, which reads: "In its relations with members, the Fund shall recognize that the postwar transitional period will be one of change and adjustment and *in making decisions on requests occasioned thereby* which are presented by any member *it shall give the member the benefit of any reasonable doubt"* [emphasis added]. As far as can be ascertained, neither the Fund nor any of its members has ever had occasion to invoke or apply this provision. It may thus be advisable for the Fund, at long last, to issue a formal statement that the "transitional period" in the sense of Article XIV, Section 5 has come to an end[84]—the more so since the words "on requests occasioned thereby" are devoid of any meaning in the context of Article XIV.

It may, of course, be argued that the Fund's obligation to "give the member the benefit of any reasonable doubt" is merely a paraphrase of a widely accepted principle of international law, namely, that

[81] IMF, *Annual Report, 1952*, p. 39; for text of the decision, see *ibid.*, pp. 87-90; the decision is also reproduced in IMF, *Selected Decisions*, pp. 21-24.

[82] The IMF, *Annual Report, 1952* contains on pp. 38-43 an informative description of the circumstances surrounding the adoption and of the rationale of the decision.

[83] See, for example, IMF, *Annual Report, 1952*, p. 42. The proposed Amendment of Article XIX(j) defines "gold tranche purchase" as follows: "Gold tranche purchase means a purchase by a member of the currency of another member in exchange for its own currency which does not cause the Fund's holding of the member's currency to exceed one hundred per cent of its quota . . ."; see also below p. 69.

[84] Such a declaration on the part of the Fund would leave unimpaired the right of members to avail themselves of the transitional arrangements of Art. XIV, Sec. 2, since this right is based on or may be inferred from Art. XIV, Sec. 3.

"limitations of sovereignty are not presumed."[85] This interpretation is, however, not persuasive, since the principle that "limitations of sovereignty are not presumed" is, under general principles of interpretation, applicable to all provisions of the Fund Agreement and not only to Section 5 of Article XIV.

However this may be, if it was the intention of paragraph 3 of the decision of the Executive Board of February 13, 1952, to assure a member "virtually automatic access" to the Fund's resources for drawings that would not raise the Fund's holdings of its currency to more than its quota, an express statement to this effect would have been preferable and would have been more readily understandable than the reference in the decision to "the overwhelming benefit of any doubt."

The Fund has never officially defined what is meant by "virtually automatic access" to its resources. Nevertheless, it is reasonable to infer that, in the context in which it is frequently used in the Fund, this formula is designed to assure a member that the Fund will, in principle, consider favorably specified categories of requests for drawings. At the same time, the formula implies that the Fund reserves the residual right not to engage in a particular transaction, if it is of the opinion that such transaction would be contrary to the provisions or purposes of the Fund. By contrast, a decision of the Executive Board which, in disregard of the legal safeguards provided in the Fund Agreement,[86] would generally confer "automatic" rather than "virtually automatic" access to the Fund's resources would presumably be *ultra vires.*

(ii) *Time limit for repurchases.* The Fund Agreement does not specify the period within which a member that has purchased from the Fund the currency of another member has to reverse the transaction by "repurchase" of its currency from the Fund. Paragraph 2(a) of the decision, however, provides that "The period should fall within an outside range of three to five years." In explaining the introduction of this time limit, the decision refers to "the necessity for ensuring the revolving character of the Fund's resources" and adds that,

[85] See, for example, the ruling of the Permanent Court of International Justice in the case of S. S. *Lotus* (1927): "Restrictions upon the independence of States cannot . . . be presumed." P.C.I.J. Series A, No. 10, p. 18.

[86] For a discussion of these safeguards, see above pp. 19-24. For a critical evaluation of the question of whether the proposed Amendment of Article V, Section 3(d) ensures legal automaticity of gold-tranche purchases, see below pp. 72-73.

in the view of the Board, "exchange purchased from the Fund should not remain outstanding beyond the period reasonably related to the payments problem for which it was purchased from the Fund."[87] Nevertheless, paragraph 2(d) of the decision holds out the assurance that the Fund will consider extensions of time, when unforeseen circumstances beyond the member's control would make unreasonable the application of the time limits set forth in paragraph 2(a) of the decision.[88]

### (c) *Creditworthiness of Members*

The decision quotes, in paragraph 1, a statement by the Managing Director (Mr. Rooth) which is designated therein as "the framework of his discussions with members on use of the Fund's resources." In this statement, Mr. Rooth advanced the view that the Fund should pay attention to a member's general creditworthiness, particularly its record with the Fund; and added that in this respect the member's record of prudence in drawing, its willingness to offer voluntary repayment when the situation permitted, and its promptness in fulfilling the obligation to transmit data on monetary reserves would be important.[89]

### (d) *Gold-tranche Policy*

Beginning with 1952, the expressions "transactions within the 'gold tranche,'"[90] "drawings within the so-called 'gold tranche,'"[91] and "policy of the Fund with respect to drawings in the so-called 'gold tranche,'"[92] have been used in Executive Board decisions and Annual Reports of the Fund.

Considering that the original Articles of Agreement do not contain any express reference to "gold tranche" (or to its antonym "credit tranche"),[93] clarification of these and related terms appears desirable.

[87] IMF, *Annual Report, 1952*, p. 88.
[88] Paragraph 2(d) of the decision refers to "the principles set forth in paragraph 2 above," although subparagraph (d) itself constitutes an integral part of paragraph 2. Reference should presumably have been made in paragraph 2(d) to the principles set forth in paragraph 2(a), (b), and (c) of this decision.
[89] IMF, *Annual Report, 1952*, p. 87.
[90] See, for example, paragraph 6 of Executive Board decision No. 155-(52/57) of October 1, 1952, relating to Stand-By Credit-Arrangements in IMF, *Selected Decisions*, p. 25.
[91] *Ibid.*; see also IMF, *Annual Report, 1952*, p. 42.
[92] See paragraph 6 of the Executive Board decision cited above in footnote 90.
[93] The proposed Amendment of Article XIX(j) contains, as previously mentioned, a definition of "gold-tranche purchase"; see above footnote 83.

(i) *"Gold tranche" as synonym for "gold subscription."* In Fund parlance the term "gold tranche" is used either as synonym for "gold subscription" or as antonym to "credit tranche." The term "gold subscription,"[94] in turn, may refer either (1) to the "initial gold subscription" of a member, or (2) to the sum of successive gold-subscription payments which comprise a member's "initial gold subscription" plus the subsequent "quota-increase gold subscription" or "quota-increase gold subscriptions," depending on whether the member's quota has been increased once or more than once.

The amount payable as initial gold subscription may or may not equal 25 per cent of quota. Original members were required to pay in gold either 25 per cent of quota or 10 per cent of their net official holdings of gold and United States dollars as of September 12, 1946 [Article III, Section 3(b)].[95] The amount payable by other than original members in gold is prescribed in the relevant paragraph of the Membership Resolution. This amount may be expressed as a specified percentage of quota (25 per cent or less), as a specified amount,[96] or the prospective member may be required to pay as gold subscription 10 per cent of its net official holdings of gold and convertible currencies.[97]

By contrast, in respect to quota increases *all* members, regardless of their initial gold subscription, are required to pay 25 per cent of the increase in gold and the balance in their currency, either by virtue of Article III, Section 4(a) or under the relevant clause of the Resolution of the Board of Governors authorizing general or individual quota increases.[98]

[94] The term "gold subscription" is used in clause E-1 of the Fund's Rules and Regulations; see IMF, *By-Laws and Rules and Regulations*, 26th Issue (Washington: 1966), p. 21.

[95] The provision of Art. III, Sec. 3(b) was also applicable to those members that joined the Fund not later than December 31, 1946 pursuant to Resolution IM-9 of the Board of Governors.

[96] See, for example, paragraph 4(a) of Resolution No. 16-9 (Membership for the Republic of Senegal) of the Board of Governors of September 20, 1961, in IMF, *Summary Proceedings, 1961*, p. 200.

[97] See, for example, Resolution No. 18-11 (Membership for the Malagasy Republic) of the Board of Governors of August 20, 1963. Under paragraph 3 of this Resolution, the Malagasy Republic shall pay in gold the smaller of (i) 25 per cent of its quota of US $15 million or (ii) 10 per cent of its net official holdings of gold and convertible currencies as of the date the Malagasy Republic makes the representation to the Fund that it has taken all action necessary to adhere to the Articles of Agreement. (IMF, *Summary Proceedings, 1963*, p. 250.)

[98] For a synopsis of individual and general quota increases in the period 1947 to 1963, see Aufricht, *The International Monetary Fund*, Appendix III, pp. 83-87.

In other words, the gold tranche, comprising the initial gold subscription and, where appropriate, the quota-increase gold subscription or subscriptions, will be equivalent to 25 per cent of quota only if (1) the member's initial quota subscription amounted to 25 per cent of quota and (2) the member's initial gold subscription plus the subsequent quota-increase gold subscriptions amounted to 25 per cent of the member's quota. If, on the other hand, (1) the initial gold subscription is smaller than 25 per cent of quota and (2) the member has decided to pay the quota-increase gold subscription in instalments but has not completed the quota-increase payment, the gold tranche or gold subscription will be correspondingly smaller.

(ii) *"Gold tranche" as antonym to "credit tranche."* In Fund parlance, the word "gold tranche" is often used as an antonym to "credit tranche." The latter term has generally been used by the Fund in reference to four equal segments of a member's quota, which represent drawing rights above the quota level. Normally, references to drawings in the first, second, third, or fourth credit tranche designate drawings by a member that bring the Fund's holdings of the member's currency to not more than 125 per cent, 150 per cent, 175 per cent, or 200 per cent of its quota.[99]

(iii) *Two versions of gold-tranche policy.* Two versions of the Fund's gold-tranche policy may be distinguished: (1) the gold-tranche policy in the strict sense, that is, virtual automaticity for drawings that do not exceed the gold subscription; and (2) the gold-tranche policy in the broader sense, which extends the principle of virtual automaticity to those drawings by a member which do not increase the Fund's holdings of its currency beyond the amount of its quota.

The rationale of the gold-tranche policy in the strict sense is presumably to assure members that they are almost automatically entitled to obtain from the Fund, against payment of their currency, the currency of other members, so long as such drawings do not exceed the equivalent of the gold subscription of the purchasing

[99] For the expression "amounts not more than twenty-five percent in excess of the quota," see Art. V, Sec. 8(c); see also, for example, IMF, *Annual Report, 1963*, p. 44 (Table 8. Credit Tranche Positions of Members of the International Monetary Fund, End of Calendar Years, 1958-62). The assumption that the four segments of the credit tranche are equal to one-fourth of the member's quota applies only so long as the Fund's holdings of a member's currency may not exceed 200 per cent of its quota. On the Fund's willingness to permit drawings beyond this point, see IMF, *Annual Report, 1963*, p. 44, footnote 6.

member.[100] The gold-tranche policy in the broader sense also authorizes a member to draw virtually automatically on the Fund in amounts that do not increase the Fund's holdings of its currency beyond the amount of its quota. However, drawings under this policy may actually have only a very tenuous connection with the gold subscription. To illustrate: suppose member A has an initial gold subscription equivalent to 3 per cent of its quota and that A has had no quota increase; suppose, furthermore, that the Fund's holdings of A's currency have been reduced to 30 per cent as a result of the purchase of A's currency from the Fund by another member. In these circumstances, a drawing by A, equivalent to 70 per cent of its quota, would be in the purview of the gold-tranche policy in the broader sense, although only an amount of 3 per cent of quota would in this case correspond to A's initial gold subscription.

In this context, Article VI, Section 2, may be cited. It provides that a member eligible to use the Fund's resources shall be entitled to purchase the currency of another member "for any purpose, including capital transfers" if the Fund's holdings of that member's currency have remained below 75 per cent of its quota during the previous six months. Drawings under this provision, that is, drawings that do not bring the Fund's holdings of the purchasing member's currency above 75 per cent of quota, are occasionally referred to as drawings within the "super gold tranche."[101]

(d) *Credit-tranche Policy*

The Fund's *Annual Report, 1955* stated that in practice the Fund's attitude toward applications for drawings within the first credit tranche (that is, drawings that raise the Fund's holdings of a member's currency above 100 per cent but not over 125 per cent of its

---

[100] One passage in the IMF, *Annual Report, 1958*, p. 23, for example, may be understood as reference to what has been designated above as "gold-tranche policy in the strict sense." It reads: "The Executive Board's decision of February 13, 1952 on Use of the Fund's resources indicated that for drawings within the 'gold tranche,' i.e., the portion of a member's quota which can be regarded as equivalent to its gold subscription . . ." Unfortunately even this statement is not free from ambiguity when it defines "gold tranche" as that portion of the member's quota which can be *regarded as*—but not necessarily *is*—equivalent to the gold subscription.

[101] The IMF, *Annual Report, 1968* defines, on p. 16, the term "super gold tranche" as the "amount by which 75 per cent of a member's quota exceeds the Fund's holdings of its currency."

*31*

quota) "is a liberal one."[102] The purpose of this declaration was to assure members that they can "confidently expect a favorable response" to applications for drawings within the first credit tranche "provided that they are also themselves making reasonable efforts to solve their problems."[103] For drawings that would bring the Fund's holdings of the purchasing member's currency above 125 per cent of its quota, "substantial justification is required," and among the justifications foreseen are transactions in support of the establishment or maintenance of convertibility.[104]

As regards the Fund's policy toward requests for drawings within the first credit tranche, it should be clear that implementation of this policy in respect of direct purchases by members of the currency of other members may in individual cases be tantamount to a waiver, under Article V, Section 4, of the conditions governing the use of the Fund's resources provided in Article V, Section 3. Such a waiver may be involved, for example, where a member has paid 25 per cent of its quota in gold and has had no prior exchange transaction with the Fund. If such a member requests a drawing amounting to 50 per cent of its quota—comprising the equivalent of its gold tranche plus another 25 per cent of its quota—and the Fund complies with the request, this transaction will result, within a period of twelve months, in an increase of the Fund's holdings of the purchasing member's currency by 50 per cent rather than 25 per cent, as contemplated in Article V, Section 3 (a)(iii). Moreover, in respect of drawings within the first credit tranche, the Fund does not in practice prescribe any specific terms and conditions to safeguard its interests, nor does it require the pledge of collateral security, a requirement authorized under Article V, Section 4, so long as the member "asking for assistance can show that it is making reasonable efforts to solve its own problems."[105]

(e) *Stand-By Arrangements*

Beginning with 1952, drawings by members under so-called stand-by arrangements have been authorized by the Fund. The general framework for stand-by arrangements has been formulated in several

[102] IMF, *Annual Report, 1955*, p. 85.
[103] IMF, *Annual Report, 1958*, p. 23.
[104] Statement by Per Jacobsson, Managing Director of the International Monetary Fund, in IMF, *Summary Proceedings, 1957*, pp. 14-15.
[105] *Ibid.*

decisions of the Executive Board.[106] Individual stand-by arrangements are in practice embodied in two documents, one entitled, for example, "Stand-By Arrangement—Peru," and the other a related statement setting forth the exchange, credit, and fiscal policies the member intends to pursue during the period of the stand-by arrangement. The texts of these two documents are not released by the Fund, but the amounts committed to members under stand-by arrangements are regularly published by the Fund.

Under a stand-by arrangement a member is assured, subject to the terms of the arrangement, that it is entitled during a fixed period to purchase from the Fund the currency or currencies of other members up to specified amounts. The amounts a member may draw under these arrangements may be limited (1) to the portion of the quota which the member would be permitted to draw under Article V, Section 3 of the Fund Agreement[107] (that is, 25 per cent of quota during any twelve-month period), or (2) to the amounts specified in accordance with the waiver provision of Article V, Section 4.

Under the first general decision on the subject, stand-by arrangements were limited to periods not exceeding six months. A subsequent decision of the Executive Board provides that the Fund will give sympathetic consideration to a request for a stand-by arrangement for a period of more than six months, if this appears warranted by the particular payments problem of the member making the request.[108] In recent Fund practice, virtually all stand-by arrangements have been concluded for twelve-month periods.

In practice, the member is authorized to terminate the stand-by arrangement at any time before the end of the specified period. The Fund, on its part, may suspend the drawing rights of the member under the arrangement (1) if, after the effective date, the member

[106] See the Executive Board decisions on Stand-By Arrangements: No. 155-(52/57) of October 1, 1952; No. 270-(53/95) of December 23, 1953; No. 876-(59/15) of April 27, 1959; decision No. 1151-(61/6) of February 20, 1961; and No. 1345-(62/23) of May 23, 1962.

[107] A member will elect to enter a stand-by arrangement with the Fund rather than engage in a direct purchase of an equivalent amount from the Fund when its primary interest is the assurance of having specified resources available, if and when the member chooses to draw, rather than in the immediate acquisition of these resources.

[108] Compare paragraph 1 of the Executive Board decision No. 155-(52/57) of October 1, 1952, with paragraph II.1 of the Executive Board decision No. 270-(53/95) of December 23, 1953, in IMF, *Selected Decisions*, p. 24 and pp. 26-27.

becomes ineligible to use the Fund's resources by virtue of the relevant provisions of the Fund Agreement,[109] or (2) as the result of a decision of the Executive Directors to consider a proposal by the Managing Director or by any Executive Director to suppress or to limit the eligibility of the member. After a member has received notice from the Fund of its total or partial ineligibility, purchases under the stand-by arrangement may be resumed by that member only after consultation between the Fund and the member and after agreement has been reached between them on the terms for the resumption of such purchases.

The drawing rights of the member under stand-by arrangements are also suspended whenever the Executive Board decides under Article XVI, Section 1(a)(ii) to suspend transactions generally. In this case it may reasonably be assumed that purchases by the member may not be resumed so long as the general suspension of transactions obtains.

Moreover, the member usually declares—either in the stand-by arrangement or in an accompanying letter or memorandum—that it will not request purchases under the arrangement if it has not observed or is not observing certain specified policies. In such a contingency, the member is obliged to consult the Fund and reach agreement with the Fund on the terms for further purchases.

## (f) Compensatory Financing of Export Fluctuations

On February 27, 1963, the Executive Board adopted a decision on the financing of deficits arising out of export shortfalls, particularly of member countries that export primary products.[110] Under this decision, members were advised that they can expect their requests for drawings to be met if the Fund finds (1) that the shortfall in export earnings is of a short-term character and is largely attributable to circumstances beyond the control of the member, and (2) that the member will cooperate with the Fund in an effort to find, where required, appropriate solutions for its balance-of-payments difficulties.

The special drawings available to members under the 1963 decision were normally not to exceed 25 per cent of the member's quota. Un-

---

[109] On ineligibility to use the Fund's resources, see above pp. 22-23.

[110] Decision No. 1477-(63/8) of February 27, 1963, IMF, *Selected Decisions*, pp. 40-43. See also *Compensatory Financing of Export Fluctuations: A Report by the International Monetary Fund* (Washington: February 1963).

der the amending decision of September 20, 1966,[111] such drawings may amount to 50 per cent of the member's quota, provided, however, that (1) except in the case of shortfalls resulting from disasters or major emergencies, such drawings may not increase the Fund's holdings of the purchasing member's currency by more than 25 per cent of quota during any 12-month period, and (2) requests for drawings beyond 25 per cent of quota under paragraph 5 of the decision will be met by the Fund only if the Fund is satisfied that the member has been cooperating with the Fund in an effort to find, where necessary, appropriate solutions for its balance-of-payments difficulties.[112]

The actual export shortfall shall be determined by comparison with the latest 12-month period preceding the drawing request on the basis of statistical data which the Fund considers sufficient for computing the amount of such shortfall.

The decision also provides that the Fund will be prepared to waive for the purpose of this program the requirement of Article V, Section 3(a)(iii) that the Fund's holdings of the purchasing member's currency may not exceed 200 per cent of that member's quota.[113]

Finally, the 1966 Compensatory Financing Decision expressly states that it is intended to supplement the Fund's gold-tranche and credit-tranche policies rather than to supersede them in respect of the members availing themselves of the facilities afforded by the program.[114]

### (g) Automatic or Conditional Drawing Rights, 1952-1968

Even if one infers, by way of a primarily textual interpretation, that all drawing rights of members have been formulated in the Fund Agreement as conditional drawing rights[115] and even if one takes note of the discretionary powers conferred by the Articles of Agree-

[111] Decision No. 2192-(66/81) of September 20, 1966; for text, see IMF, *Annual Report, 1967*, pp. 159-161. On actual drawings under the 1963 and 1966 decisions, see *ibid.*, p. 49. See also *Compensatory Financing of Export Fluctuations: A Second Report by the International Monetary Fund* (Washington: September 1966).

[112] See paragraph 5 of decision No. 2192-(66/81), in IMF, *Annual Report, 1967*, p. 159.

[113] See paragraph 10 of decision No. 2192-(66/81), *ibid.*, p. 160.

[114] The respective passage in paragraph 10 reads as follows: "Moreover, the Fund will apply its tranche policies to drawing requests by a member as if the Fund's holdings of the member's currency were less than its actual holdings of that currency by the amount of any drawings outstanding under paragraph (5)."

[115] See above, especially pp. 19-25.

ment on the Fund in matters relating to the exercise by members of their drawing rights, one will have to admit that the dialogue between the advocates of automatic and those of conditional drawing rights did not end at Bretton Woods in 1944. On the contrary, the Fund's "gold-tranche policy," both in its strict and in its broader sense,[116] and the decisions of the Fund's Executive Board on Compensatory Financing of Export Fluctuations,[117] are probably more readily understandable in their historical setting, if one considers them as inroads by the advocates of "automatic" or "quasi-automatic" drawing rights into the originally all-embracing sphere of conditional drawing rights.

By contrast, the credit-tranche policy of the Fund and the terms and conditions prescribed by the Fund under stand-by arrangements, usually in conjunction with a waiver of conditions under Article V, Section 4, evidence the conditional character of drawing rights. In particular, the statement that the Fund's attitude toward applications for drawings within the first credit tranche is a *liberal* one, *"provided* that they [the drawing members] are also themselves making reasonable efforts to solve their problems," may in individual instances turn out to be less liberal than the relevant provisions of the Fund Agreement. To illustrate: suppose member A, with a gold subscription equal to 25 per cent of quota, has made its first drawing in an amount equivalent to 25 per cent of quota twelve months prior to its second request for a drawing. That member would be *entitled,* under Article V, Section 3(a)(iii) of the Fund Agreement, to draw from the Fund the currency of another member in amounts not exceeding 25 per cent of quota, subject only to two exceptions: that the member is not ineligible to use the Fund's resources[118] and that the currency to be purchased has not formally been declared a scarce currency pursuant to Article VII, Section 3. But Article V, Section 3 does *not* enumerate among the conditions governing the use of the Fund's resources the requirement that the purchasing member has to show that it is making reasonable efforts "to solve its own problems."[119]

---

[116] See above, pp. 28-31.

[117] See above, pp. 34-35.

[118] See, on this point, Art. V, Sec. 3(a)(iv).

[119] There is, of course, the provision of Art. IV, Sec. 4(a), which reads: "Each member undertakes to collaborate with the Fund to promote exchange stability, to maintain orderly exchange arrangements with other members, and to avoid competitive exchange alterations." But this provision applies to every member irrespective of whether or not it is using the Fund's resources.

Where drawings in the second, third, and fourth credit tranche are involved, the requirement of the relevant policy statement that "substantial justification is required"—including presumably evidence that the member is adopting appropriate measures to safeguard its external financial position—adds a new and more stringent condition in those situations where no waiver of conditions under Article V, Section 4 of the Fund Agreement is required. Where, on the other hand, a waiver of such conditions is called for, the above-mentioned statement on credit-tranche policy does not add any legal requirement over and above those provided in the Fund Agreement. Actually, it may be argued that the credit-tranche requirement of "substantial justification" is in itself not more stringent, or for that matter not more efficacious, than the waiver provision of Article V, Section 4, which empowers the Fund "in its discretion, *and on terms which safeguard its interests* [to] waive any of the conditions prescribed in Section 3(a)" (Emphasis added).

## IV. THE ROLE OF GOLD IN THE FUND AGREEMENT

### 1. WAS THE GOLD STANDARD ABOLISHED IN THE 1930's?

For more than three decades it has been fashionable in many quarters to speak of the abolition or the breakdown in the 1930's of "the" gold standard. However, the monetary units of many countries are still defined in terms of gold; gold still serves as a means of settlement of international transactions between monetary authorities.

What, then, has actually happened? To visualize more precisely what happened to the legal status of gold in the 1930's in most countries of the world, and more particularly in Europe, it will be helpful to remember these facts: (1) The statutory link between the monetary unit and the price of gold was discontinued in most countries.[120] (2) The statutory obligation of central banks to redeem paper money in gold was abolished or suspended. (3) The central banks, which since the early 1920's had adopted note-cover provisions requiring them to hold only part of their monetary reserves in gold and the remainder in foreign exchange, incurred heavy losses in their foreign-exchange assets as a result of the devaluation of major reserve currencies.[121] (4) Many countries declared "gold-coin" or "gold-value" clauses in domestic or international contracts invalid.[122] Thus, four major characteristics or determinants of the monetary status of gold had become either expressly outlawed or had lapsed in practice.

Nevertheless, gold was still in demand as a reserve asset of central banks and of the newly established exchange-stabilization funds.[123]

[120] In the United Kingdom, for example, subsection (2) of Section 1 of the Gold Standard Act, 1925 (15 & 16 Geo. 5, ch. 29) was repealed by subsection (1) of Section 1 of the Gold Standard (Amendment) Act, 1931 (21 & 22 Geo. 5, ch. 46), with the result that the obligation of the Bank of England to sell to any person, against payment in legal tender, gold bullion of approximately 400 oz. troy of fine gold at the price of £3.17s. 10 1/2d per standard ounce of gold, eleven-twelfths fine, was suspended. On the Gold Standard Act of 1925, see generally A. E. Feavearyear, *The Pound Sterling: A History of English Money* (Oxford: The Clarendon Press, 1931), pp. 325-328.

[121] For information on the reduction of the foreign-exchange reserves of selected central banks in 1931 and 1932, see League of Nations, *International Currency Experience* (Princeton: 1944), pp. 39-41.

[122] On judicial and legislative restriction of gold clauses, see Arthur Nussbaum, *Money in the Law: National and International* (Brooklyn: Foundation Press, 1950), pp. 262-299.

[123] On the transfer of central banking functions to exchange-stabilization funds, see League of Nations, *International Currency Experience* (Princeton: 1944), pp. 158-159.

## 2. The Par-Value Regime of the Fund Agreement

### (a) Par Value of Monetary Unit of Members

Each member of the Fund is expected, in agreement with the Fund, to define the initial par value of its currency in accordance with Article IV, Section 1(a) of the Fund Agreement. That is, the member is to express the parity price of its monetary unit in terms of a specified quantity of gold as a common denominator or in terms of the U.S. dollar of the weight and fineness in effect on July 1, 1944.[124]

This provision of the Fund Agreement is in line with the old practice of many governments of defining their monetary units in terms of gold or other monetary units. However, not all members of the Fund that have agreed with the Fund on a par value of their monetary unit have corresponding statutory provisions in force. As regards the legal relationship between the par value which a member may have duly established for its currency under the Fund Agreement and the corresponding domestic statutory law, the following situations may be distinguished: (1) A country may have a statutory definition of its monetary unit in terms of gold that is in substance identical with the corresponding definition of the par value under the Fund Agreement. The United States[124] and Belgium[125] may be mentioned as examples. (2) A country may have abandoned a formerly statutory price of gold but nevertheless have a par value agreed with the Fund. The United Kingdom is an example. (3) A country may have retained on its statute books a definition of its monetary unit, but this definition may, in effect, have been superseded by the par value agreed with the Fund. Norway can serve as an example.[126]

### (b) Change of Par Value

The Fund Agreement contains several provisions on the objectives of par-value changes and prescribes the procedures to be observed by the member and the Fund in adopting such changes. A member shall not propose a change in the par value of its currency except to correct a fundamental disequilibrium [Article IV, Section 5(a)]. A change in the par value of a member's currency may be made only on

---

[124] See below, p. 47.

[125] See Art. 1 of the Monetary Law, 1957 of Belgium, as reproduced in Hans Aufricht, *Central Banking Legislation, volume II. Europe* (Washington: International Monetary Fund, 1967), p. 99.

[126] See Art. 1 of the Monetary Act, 1875 of Norway, *ibid.*, p. 529.

the proposal of that member and after consultation with the Fund [Article IV, Section 5(b)]. A member, though obliged to consult the Fund on any change, is not required to seek approval for changes not exceeding 10 per cent of the initial par value [Article IV, Section 5(c)(i)].[127] For any change in par value that exceeds 10 per cent but is not in excess of 20 per cent of the initial par value, the member is obliged to seek the approval of the Fund,[128] and the Fund shall declare its attitude within 72 hours, if the member so requests [Article IV, Section 5(c)(ii)]. On other proposals by a member to change the par value of its monetary unit, the Fund is not bound to take action within such a 72-hour period.[129]

Although, under Article IV, Section 5(b), a change in a par value may be made only on the proposal of the member concerned, uniform changes in par value may be decided on by the Fund by a majority of the total voting power of all members.[130] A decision on a "uniform" change of par values is binding on all members except those that notify the Fund within 72 hours of the decision that they do not wish the par value of their currencies changed.[131]

A historical survey of the changes of par values proposed by members in the period December 1946 to February 1968 is outside the scope of this study. Information on changes in par values may be found in the Fund's *Annual Report* and in the *Schedule of Par Values*, issued by the Fund from time to time.[132]

[127] Under Art. IV, Sec. 5(e), however, a member may change the par value of its currency without the concurrence of the Fund, if the change does not affect the international transactions of members of the Fund.

[128] Art. IV, Sec. 5(c)(ii).

[129] Art. IV, Sec. 5(c)(iii). On the economic effects of devaluation, see Fritz Machlup, "Relative Prices and Aggregate Spending in the Analysis of Devaluation," *American Economic Review*, vol. 45 (June 1955), pp. 255-278.

[130] Art. IV, Sec. 7 provides: "Notwithstanding the provisions of Section 5(b) of this Article, the Fund by a majority of the total voting power may make uniform proportionate changes in the par values of the currencies of all members, provided each such change is approved by every member which has 10 percent or more of the total of the quotas." At present, only the quotas of the United Kingdom and of the United States amount to more than 10 per cent of the total quotas of all members.

[131] Under the proposed Amendment of Art. IV, Sec. 7, an 85 per cent majority of the total voting power is required for uniform proportionate changes in the par values of the currencies of all members; see below p. 66.

[132] See, for example, IMF, *Schedule of Par Values*, 46th Issue, August 15, 1968. The first *Schedule of Par Values* was released by the Fund on December 18, 1946. See also Margaret G. de Vries, "Fund Members' Adherence to the Par Value Regime: Empirical Evidence," IMF, *Staff Papers*, vol. XIII (November 1966), pp. 504-532.

A corollary of the requirement that members agree with the Fund on a par value of their currency in terms of gold is the provision of Article IV, Section 2, which obligates members (1) not to buy gold at a price above par value plus the margin prescribed by the Fund, and (2) not to sell gold at a price below par value minus the margin prescribed by the Fund.[133] This provision is addressed to *members* and, in particular, to their *monetary authorities* (central banks, stabilization funds, or treasuries); it covers gold transactions of monetary authorities with one another or with private persons. However, Article IV, Section 2 does not preclude transactions between private persons (that is, persons other than monetary authorities) at prices that differ from the par value by more than the margins prescribed by the Fund.

The communiqué issued in Washington on March 17, 1968, by the governors of the central banks of Belgium, Germany, Italy, the Netherlands, Switzerland,[134] the United Kingdom, and the United States[135] is presumably designed to reaffirm the rule of Article IV, Section 2, when it states:

> The governors agreed to cooperate fully to maintain the existing parities as well as orderly conditions in their exchange markets in accordance with their obligations under the Articles of Agreement of the International Monetary Fund. The governors believe that henceforth officially held gold should be used only to effect transfers among monetary authorities, and, therefore, they decide no longer to supply gold to the London gold market or any other gold market. Moreover, as the existing stock of monetary gold is sufficient in view of the prospective establishment of the facility for special drawing rights, they no longer feel it necessary to buy gold from the market. Finally, they agreed that henceforth they will not sell gold to monetary authorities to replace gold sold in private markets.

It may be inferred from this statement that transfers of gold among monetary authorities will continue to take place at $35 per ounce. For

[133] The permissible margin above and below par value for transactions in gold by members has been set forth in Rule F-4 of the Fund's Rules and Regulations. This margin may not exceed 1 per cent of par value. For alternative computations of the permissible margins, see Rule F-4(1).

[134] Switzerland is not a member of the IMF.

[135] The communiqué reflects agreement reached among the governors of the seven central banks who attended the meeting in Washington on March 16 and 17, 1968. The last paragraph of the communiqué reads: "The governors invite the cooperation of other central banks in the policies set forth above."

transactions on behalf of persons other than monetary authorities, however, the communiqué establishes a new regime for gold markets and, in particular, for the London gold market.[136] While in the period 1961 to March 1968 transactions in the London gold market took place at uniform prices for official and private accounts, under the regime envisaged in the communiqué of March 17, 1968, gold may be purchased or sold by private persons in the London or other gold markets at prices that differ, however widely, from the par value of currencies in terms of gold.

### (c) *Value Guarantee of the Fund's Holdings of the Currencies of Members*

Normally, all computations relating to currencies of members when applying the provisions of the Fund Agreement shall be made in terms of the par values of the monetary units of the members concerned [Article IV, Section 1(b)]. However, this rule does not apply if the Fund finds, pursuant to Article IV, Section 8(b), that the foreign-exchange value of a member's monetary unit has depreciated to a significant extent within the member's territories.[137]

Under Article IV, Section 8(a), the gold value of the Fund's assets shall be maintained "notwithstanding changes in the par or foreign exchange value of the currency of any member."

The Fund Agreement provides that normally the gold value of the basic monetary unit of members of the Fund will be fixed in terms of a specified weight of gold (1) by agreement between the member and the Fund on an initial par value[138] or (2) as result of a change in par value under Article IV, Section 5. The Fund Agreement envisages further that the "gold content" of the U.S. dollar will either

---

[136] On the London gold pool, see "The London Gold Market," *Bank of England. Quarterly Bulletin,* vol. IV (1964), pp. 16-21.

[137] In Fund practice computations are made in terms of the par value, except as regards the currencies of Algeria, Argentina, Bolivia, Brazil, Cameroon, Central African Republic, Chad, Chile, Colombia, Congo (Brazzaville), Congo (Kinshasa), Dahomey, Gabon, Guinea, Indonesia, Ivory Coast, Korea, Malagasy Republic, Mali, Mauritania, Nepal, Niger, Paraguay, Peru, Upper Volta, Venezuela, Viet-Nam. The rates of computations by the Fund involving the currencies of the above listed members are published monthly in the respective country pages of IMF, *International Financial Statistics.*

[138] Original members of the Fund are expected to agree on an initial par value pursuant to Art. IV, Sec. 1(a) and Art. XX, Sec. 4. Other members of the Fund are expected to agree on an initial par value pursuant to §5 of the respective Membership Resolution.

remain fixed at 0.888 671 grams of fine gold[139] or, in the event of a change pursuant to Article IV, Section 5, will be fixed in terms of another specified weight of gold.

Even in the event of a so-called "uniform change of par values" it is presumed that the gold value of the Fund's assets will be determined by reference to par values expressed in specified weights of gold. However, the Fund is empowered, under Article IV, Section 8(d), at the time when a uniform proportionate change in the par values of all members is proposed "to decide otherwise." However, no uniform change of par values has been proposed up to now (April 1969).

Under Article IV, Section 8(b), a member is required to pay to the Fund within a reasonable time "an amount of its currency equal to the reduction in the gold value of its currency held by the Fund" whenever the par value of a member's monetary unit is reduced. Conversely, whenever the par value of a member's monetary unit is increased the Fund is required, under Article IV, Section 8(c), to return to that member within a reasonable time an amount of its currency equal to the increase in the gold value of that currency held by the Fund. Moreover, Article IV, Section 8(b) requires a member to make equalizing payments to the Fund whenever "the foreign exchange value of a member's currency has, in the opinion of the Fund, depreciated to a significant extent within the member's territories." In other words, any significant depreciation of the foreign-exchange value of a member's monetary unit may, even in the absence of a change in par value, oblige a member to make payments in its currency in order to maintain the gold value of the Fund's holdings of that currency.[140]

(d) *Par Value and Foreign-Exchange Rates*

Within the foreign-exchange-rate regime provided for in the Articles of Agreement of the International Monetary Fund, foreign-exchange rates for transactions in the currencies of members taking place in their territories shall be based on the par value within the margins

[139] The weight and fineness of the United States dollar in effect on July 1, 1944 is 0.888 671 grams of fine gold, referred to in Art. IV, Sec. 1(a) of the Fund Agreement.

[140] On application of Art. IV, Sec. 8 to computations by the Fund in respect of fluctuating currencies, see Executive Board decision No. 321-(54/32) of June 15, 1954 and the related decisions No. 1245-(61/45) of August 4, 1961 and No. 1283-(61/56) of December 20, 1961 in IMF, *Selected Decisions*, pp. 8-12.

prescribed by Article IV, Section 3, unless different margins have been approved by the Fund or are authorized under the Fund Agreement.[141]

As regards spot-exchange transactions, members may, under Article IV, Section 3(i) of the Fund Agreement, permit in their territories selling and buying rates for the currencies of other members within a range of 1 per cent either side of the par value. (All rates within these margins may be designated as "parity rates.") This does not preclude, however, that the rate at which foreign-exchange transactions are settled equals the par value. (Such rates may be designated as "par-value rates.") Accordingly, whenever transactions take place at parity rates, but not at the par-value rate, the par value is not tantamount to a foreign-exchange rate. It merely furnishes the "base price" on which, for purposes of Article IV, Section 3, the maximum and minimum rates of exchange are determined. If, however, foreign-exchange transactions take place at the par-value rate, the par value (in addition to defining the basic monetary unit of the currency or currencies of members and of defining the unit of account of the Fund) is the equivalent of the foreign-exchange rate of the currency involved.[142]

The major provisions of the Fund Agreement relating to foreign-exchange rates for transactions in the currencies of members taking place in their territories may be briefly indicated as follows: (1) Selling and buying rates for spot-exchange transactions shall not deviate from the par value by more than 1 per cent [Article IV, Section 3(i)].[143] (2) Selling and buying rates for other than spot-exchange transactions shall not deviate from the par value by a wider margin than the Fund considers reasonable [Article IV, Section 3(ii)]. (3) Each

[141] On Fund jurisdiction in respect of multiple-currency practices, see Art. VIII, Sec. 3 and Art. XIV, Sec. 2 of the Fund Agreement.

[142] In such a situation the Fund's Schedule of Par Values takes on the character of a schedule of foreign-exchange rates.

[143] On July 24, 1959, the Executive Board adopted decision No. 904-(59/32) on "Exchange Dealings and Margins under Conditions of Increasing Convertibility." It reads as follows: "The Fund does not object to exchange rates which are within 2 per cent of parity for spot exchange transactions between a member's currency and the currencies of other members taking place within the member's territories, whenever such rates result from the maintenance of margins of no more than 1 per cent from parity for a convertible, including externally convertible, currency." This decision is based on Art. VIII, Sec. 3 of the Fund Agreement, which empowers the Fund to approve multiple-currency practices. It authorizes in effect a widening to 2 per cent of the 1 per cent margin prescribed for spot-exchange transactions in Art. IV, Sec. 3(i), provided that at least one of the currencies involved in the transaction is a convertible currency.

member undertakes to ensure by appropriate measures, consistent with the Fund Agreement, that within its territories foreign-exchange transactions between its currency and the currencies of other members take place only within the limits prescribed in Article IV, Section 3.[144] (4) Members whose monetary authorities freely buy and sell gold within the limits prescribed in Article IV, Section 2 of the Fund Agreement for the settlement of international transactions are deemed to comply with the above-mentioned obligations of members [Article IV, Section 4(b)].[145] (5) The introduction of multiple exchange rates generally requires the approval of the Fund (Article VIII, Section 3). These provisions of the Fund Agreement significantly supplement domestic measures on exchange rates in central bank and monetary laws, since they generally limit the discretion of monetary authorities in regard to exchange-rate measures. At the same time, they reflect a basic assumption of the Fund Agreement, namely, that exchange-rate matters are not considered to be exclusively within the domestic jurisdiction of the members, but of international concern.[146]

From the purposes and provisions of the Fund Agreement it may be inferred that the following foreign-exchange-rate pattern is considered the most desirable one: (1) *fixed rates*, as opposed to fluctuating rates; (2) *single (uniform) rates*, as opposed to multiple rates; and (3) *rates that can be maintained without exchange restrictions on current transactions.*

The Fund has jurisdiction to approve multiple exchange rates under Article VIII, Section 3,[147] and exchange restrictions on current transactions under Article VIII, Section 2 of the Fund Agreement. It may thereby legalize specified deviations from the above indicated preferred exchange-rate pattern. By contrast, the issue of whether and to what extent the Fund is legally empowered, or should be empowered, to authorize a member to maintain a fluctuating-rate regime,

---

[144] Art. IV, Sec. 4(b).

[145] On the implications of this provision in the context of United States gold policy, see below p. 49.

[146] See especially the statement by Louis Rasminsky (Canada), Reporting Delegate, in *Bretton Woods Proceedings*, vol. 1, p. 867: ". . . an exchange rate is in its very nature a two-ended thing, and . . . changes in exchange rates are therefore properly matters of international concern. . . ."

[147] For a survey of multiple exchange rates maintained by members of the Fund, see IMF, *Nineteenth Annual Report on Exchange Restrictions* (Washington: 1968).

has been hotly debated inside and outside the Fund for more than twenty years.

When the Fund in 1947 examined the multiple-currency practices of members prevailing at that time, it took cognizance of the fact that certain multiple-currency practices included fluctuating exchange rates. At that time it informed its members that, when a multiple-currency practice includes *a free market with a fluctuating rate,* the member should agree with the Fund on the scope of transactions permitted to take place in that market. Moreover, any changes in the scope of the free market should be agreed upon with the Fund. Hence, the Fund considered itself authorized to approve a *regime of fluctuating exchange rates* as a part of a pattern of multiple exchange rates.[148]

As regards single-rate systems, the Fund has stated that a "system of fluctuating exchange rates is not a satisfactory alternative to the par value system."[149] However, if a member represents that it is unable to maintain an agreed par value and that it is not in a position to select a new one immediately, the Fund may, if it finds the member's statement persuasive, make a declaration to this effect, even if it cannot formally approve a fluctuating single-rate system. In the words of the Fund's *Annual Report, 1951:* "Exceptions" to the par-value system, as a system which presupposes single and fixed rates, "can be justified under the Fund Agreement only under special circumstances and for temporary periods."[150]

### 3. GOLD-EXCHANGE-STANDARD FEATURES OF THE FUND AGREEMENT

One of the principal features of the gold-exchange standard is the holding by central banks of reserve assets in foreign exchange in lieu of or in addition to gold. If one examines the provisions of the Fund Agreement concerning gold and currency subscription, the 75 per cent level of the Fund's holdings of a member's currency, and certain aspects of the "repurchase" requirements of members, one will note certain characteristics that for purposes of this study may be designated as "gold-exchange-standard features." This terminology may further be justified on the ground that the Fund's resources have occa-

---

[148] See "Communication sent by Fund to Members on Multiple Currency Practices," dated December 19, 1947, in IMF, *Annual Report, 1948,* p. 68.

[149] IMF, *Annual Report, 1951,* p. 39.

[150] *Ibid.,* p. 41. For a reaffirmation of this view, see IMF, *Annual Report, 1962,* pp. 58-67.

sionally been designated as a "second line of reserves" or as "secondary reserves."[151]

First, it appears that ideally 25 per cent of the Fund's resources were to consist of gold, the balance of members' currencies. This assumption may explain why a member that has paid 90 per cent of its initial subscription in its currency and has not engaged in any exchange transaction with the Fund during the fiscal year of the Fund, incurs a "repurchase" obligation toward the Fund, provided its monetary reserves have sufficiently increased during that year [Article V, Section 7(b)(i)].[152]

Second, repurchase obligations must not be performed, if they were to involve a payment by member A of B's currency and if the Fund's holdings of B's currency equal at least 75 per cent of B's quota [Article V, Section 7(c)(ii)].

Third, repurchase obligations have to be discharged by payment of gold or convertible currencies—that is, in currencies of members that have notified the Fund that they do not avail themselves of the transitional arrangements of Article XIV, Section 2.

### 4. Gold Legislation and Gold Policy of the United States

#### (a) Legal Definition of the Dollar in Terms of Gold

The legal definition of the U.S. dollar in terms of gold has been incorporated by reference into the Fund Agreement, where it provides that members may express the par value of their monetary unit in terms of the U.S. dollar of the weight and fineness in effect on July 1, 1944 [Article IV, Section 1(a)]. This gold weight and fineness is that defined by Presidential Proclamation No. 2072 of January 31, 1934 (48 Stat. 1730, 31 USCA 821 note) as equalling 15-5/21 grains of gold 9/10 fine.[153]

[151] See IMF, *Annual Report, 1952*, p. 46.

[152] For further information on repurchase obligations under the Fund Agreement, see IMF, *Fund Circular No. 9, Revision 3* (Washington, June 1, 1964), p. 16. On the financial aspects of exchange transactions between members and the Fund, see generally Rudolf Kroc, *The Financial Structure of the Fund*, IMF, Pamphlet Series No. 5, 2d ed. (Washington: 1967). On the proposed Amendment of the repurchase provisions of the Fund Agreement, see below p. 67.

[153] Arthur Nussbaum, *A History of the Dollar* (New York: Columbia University Press, 1957), p. 185, remarks that under this Proclamation "the 'weight of the gold dollar' was fixed at 15 5/21 grains, 9/10 fine. There was, we know, no 'gold dollar.' It would have been more exact to fix the 'standard unit of value' at 15 5/21 grains, 9/10 fine and this is the real meaning of the proclamation."

## (b) *Nature of the U.S. Gold Standard*

There is general agreement that the United States by enacting the Gold Reserve Act, 1934, abandoned the gold-coin standard.[154] Gold coins were no longer to be minted and neither Federal Reserve notes nor gold certificates were any longer redeemable in gold. There is no general agreement whether or to what extent the monetary system should be regarded as a gold standard, especially as managed since 1936.

The practice, dating back to 1936, of selling gold bullion to and purchasing gold bullion from the monetary authorities of friendly governments at the price of $35 (minus or plus a charge of 1/4 of 1 per cent) per ounce may well be designated as a qualified gold-bullion standard. Under this arrangement only a comparatively small number of persons or entities can expect to buy gold from, or to sell gold to, the U.S. Treasury against dollars. In contradistinction, under the British gold-bullion standard (as formulated in the Gold Standard Act, 1925) the Bank of England was bound to sell to *any person* gold bars containing approximately four hundred ounces troy of fine gold against payment in legal tender.

It should be clear that the United States is, at present, the only country in the world that "freely" sells gold to the monetary authorities of other countries, and that the gold policy of the United States is based on a voluntary commitment by the United States.

The circumstances under which this commitment was originally made can be summarized briefly. On September 25, 1936, the U.S. Treasury issued an "International Declaration on Currency."[155] On the same day, similar statements were released by the British and French Governments. These parallel declarations by the three Governments constituted the so-called Tripartite Monetary Agreement.

Paragraph 2 of that declaration stated that it is a constant objective of the Government of the United States in its international monetary relations "to maintain the greatest possible equilibrium in the system of international exchange and to avoid to the utmost extent the creation of any disturbance of that system by American monetary action."[156] The declaration also expressed the view that the Government of the United States in its policy towards international monetary re-

[154] *Ibid.*, p. 185.
[155] For text of the declaration, see *Federal Reserve Bulletin* (October 1936), pp. 759-760.
[156] *Ibid.*, p. 759.

lations will take into full account the requirements of internal prosperity. The tripartite character of the declaration is reflected, for example, in a clause of the same paragraph 2, which states that the Government of the United States shares with the Governments of France and Great Britain the conviction that "this two-fold policy will serve the general purpose which all the Governments should pursue."

The Tripartite Agreement was supplemented on October 13, 1936 by an announcement of the Treasury Department "regarding sale of gold for export,"[157] which constituted, and presumably still constitutes,[158] the basis of the present policy of the United States to sell gold "freely" to the monetary authorities of friendly countries.[159] Under this declaration the Secretary of the Treasury offered to sell gold to Great Britain and France—or to earmark gold for the account of the exchange-equalization or stabilization funds of Great Britain and France—at $35 per ounce plus a handling charge of 1/4 of one per cent.[160] The Secretary, in making this offer, expressly declared that the offer might be revoked or altered at twenty-four hours notice.[161]

It appears that corresponding declarations on the part of Great Britain and France did not result in corresponding action on the part of these countries.[162]

An important corollary of the Tripartite Agreement was the establishment of working arrangements under which the United States Stabilization Fund cooperated in foreign-exchange markets with the monetary authorities of countries that did not maintain a fixed gold price. These working arrangements were regarded as beneficial to all participants.[163]

[157] *Federal Reserve Bulletin* (November 1936), p. 852.

[158] The Gold Regulations, issued under the authority of the Gold Reserve Act of 1934, that are currently in force in the United States, may be found in Title 31 of the Code of Federal Regulations, §54.

[159] The declaration supplements the announcement made by the Secretary of the Treasury on February 1, 1934 relating to the purchase of gold at $35 per ounce less 1/4 of one per cent for handling charges. For text of this declaration, see *Federal Reserve Bulletin* (February 1934), p. 69.

[160] *Federal Reserve Bulletin* (November 1936), p. 852. On November 24, 1936, the Treasury announced that the offer had been extended to the following additional countries: Belgium, the Netherlands, Switzerland.

[161] *Ibid.*

[162] See Arthur Nussbaum, A *History of the Dollar, op.cit.,* p. 205.

[163] See League of Nations. *International Currency Experience* (Princeton: 1944), pp. 147 and 159.

In retrospect, it appears that the stabilizing transactions carried on under these arrangements differed significantly from the regime governing exchange transactions between members and the Fund under the Fund Agreement. The Fund, as previously indicated, normally assumes fixed exchange rates and fixed gold prices, whereas the Tripartite Agreement assumed a fixed price in terms of gold for the U.S. dollar and fluctuating rates for the pound sterling and the French franc. Under the Tripartite Agreement the monetary authorities of the parties, including the exchange-stabilization funds, were empowered to intervene in the foreign-exchange markets on their own initiative. By contrast, the Fund's resources may generally be used only on the initiative of a member of the Fund for the purpose of supplying that member with the currency of another member in exchange for gold or the currency of the member desiring to make the exchange (Article V, Section 2).

## V. THE CHANGING SETTING

### 1. MEMBERSHIP

In the period December 27, 1945 to November 1, 1968, the number of members of the Fund increased from 22 to 111. The individual members, together with the date of signature and acceptance of the Fund Agreement, as of November 1, 1968 are listed in Appendix I.[164]

### (a) *Schedule-A Members*

For purposes of this study a "Schedule-A member" is a member that accepted the Fund Agreement not later than December 31, 1946. This category of members includes the original members and the members that accepted membership under the authority of Resolution No. IM-9 (Acceptance of Membership by Schedule-A countries), adopted on March 14, 1946, by the Inaugural Meeting of the Board of Governors of the Fund.

By December 31, 1946 there were 40 Schedule-A members, listed in the table below, comprising the 30 members that accepted membership not later than December 31, 1945 [in accordance with Article II, Section 1 and Article XX, Section 2(e)] and ten additional Schedule-A members that joined the Fund under Resolution No. IM-9 of the Board of Governors.[165]

Membership in the Fund of three of these 40 countries has ceased: Poland as of March 14, 1950; Czechoslovakia as of December 31, 1954; and Cuba as of April 2, 1960.

The Union of Soviet Socialist Republics, though listed in Schedule A, has not accepted membership in the Fund.

### (b) *Other Members*

Individual members that joined the Fund after December 31, 1946 are subject to the Articles of Agreement and the terms and conditions of the resolution of the Board of Governors of the Fund relating to the admission to membership of the country concerned. By contrast, no individual membership resolution was adopted for Schedule-A members.[166]

[164] See below, pp. 77-79.

[165] For complete text, see IMF, *Selected Documents, Board of Governors. Inaugural Meeting* (Savannah, Ga.: March 8 to 18, 1946), p. 21.

[166] Resolution IM-9, though expressly approved under Art. II, Sec. 2 of the Fund Agreement, differs in form and content from individual membership resolutions adopted by the Fund subsequent to December 31, 1946.

SCHEDULE-A MEMBERS

| Original Members | | Resolution No. IM-9 Members |
|---|---|---|
| *Members that joined IMF by Dec. 27, 1945* | *Members that joined IMF by Dec. 31, 1945* | *that joined the IMF by December 31, 1946* |
| Belgium | Chile | Brazil |
| Bolivia | Dominican Republic | Costa Rica |
| Canada | Ecuador | Cuba |
| China | Guatemala | Denmark |
| Colombia | Iran | El Salvador |
| Czechoslovakia | Mexico | Nicaragua |
| Egypt (United | Paraguay | Panama |
| Arab Republic) | Peru | Poland |
| Ethiopia | | Uruguay |
| France | | Venezuela |
| Greece | | |
| Honduras | | |
| Iceland | | |
| India | | |
| Iraq | | |
| Luxembourg | | |
| Netherlands | | |
| Norway | | |
| Philippine | | |
| Republic | | |
| South Africa | | |
| United Kingdom | | |
| United States | | |
| Yugoslavia | | |
| (22) | (8) | (10) |

In the period January 1, 1947 to September 30, 1968, another 74 countries accepted membership in the Fund under individual membership resolutions. These countries may, for the most part, be grouped under three categories as follows:

*Four countries* that, though listed in Schedule A, had not joined the Fund by December 31, 1946 and accepted membership under special membership resolutions as of the date indicated in the parentheses: Australia (August 5, 1947), Haiti (September 8, 1953), Liberia (March 28, 1962), and New Zealand (August 31, 1961).

*Eighteen countries* that were not represented at the Bretton Woods Conference: Afghanistan, Argentina, Austria, Finland, Germany, Ireland, Italy, Japan, Korea, Lebanon, Nepal, Portugal, Saudi Arabia, Spain, Sweden, Syria, Thailand, Turkey.

*Forty-six countries* whose territories were "under the authority" of Belgium, France, the Netherlands or the United Kingdom [in the sense of Article XX, Section 4(g)][167] when these four countries became members of the Fund. Subsequently, the 46 countries, released from the territorial authority of the respective metropolitan powers, accepted membership in the Fund.

The territory of at least two members—Cameroon and Togo—resulted from the merger of territories which, at the time of the Bretton Woods Conference, were separately administered by France and the United Kingdom as Class B-Mandates and later as trust territories with France and the United Kingdom as administering authorities.

The partition of India under the Indian Independence (International Arrangements) Order of 1947, resulted in the emergence of Pakistan as a separate legal entity. Under the rules adopted by the United Nations and the International Monetary Fund, Pakistan was deemed to be a new state which, in order to become a member of an international organization, had to apply for membership, while India retained its membership status in the international organizations of which she was a member on August 15, 1947.[168]

Because of their special status, prior to membership in the Fund, the territories of Libya and Somalia, and Sudan under joint Anglo-Egyptian authority, have not been included under the foregoing categories.[169]

(c) *Quotas and their Adjustment*

The total resources of the Fund derived from subscriptions by members increased from $6,772.5 million on December 27, 1945 (the day the Fund Agreement entered into force) to $21,198.45 million on November 1, 1968.[170]

This increase in the total of quotas is due in part to the adherence of new members to the Fund Agreement during this period, and in part to increases in quotas of the original and other members.

---

[167] Art. XX, Sec. 4(g) reads: "By their signature of this Agreement, all governments accept it both on their own behalf and in respect of all their colonies, overseas territories, all territories under their protection, suzerainty, or authority and all territories in respect of which they exercise a mandate."

[168] Pakistan accepted membership in the Fund effective July 11, 1950.

[169] On state succession, see Hans Aufricht, "State Succession under the Law and Practice of the International Monetary Fund," *International and Comparative Law Quarterly*, vol. 11 (January 1962), pp. 154-170.

[170] For the quotas of members as determined at the Bretton Woods Conference, see Schedule A of the Fund Agreement. For the status of quotas on November 1, 1968, see below pp. 80-85.

53

Under Article III, Section 2 of the Fund Agreement, the Fund may, at intervals of five years after the entry into force of the Agreement, propose a general adjustment of the quotas of members. The Fund may also consider at any time the adjustment of the particular quota of any member. Under the original Articles of Agreement a four-fifths majority of the total voting power is required for any change in quota, and no quota shall be changed without the consent of the member concerned. The proposed Amendment to the Articles of Agreement provides for an 85 per cent majority of the total voting power for a general review of quotas.[171]

Up to now, the Fund has only on two occasions suggested a general increase of quotas of members, namely, in 1959 and in 1965.[172]

In connection with the second quinquennial review of quotas which the Executive Directors completed in January 1956, no general increase in quotas was proposed, but the quotas of a number of small countries were found to be particularly inadequate. As a result of the review it was understood that requests for increases in small quotas would be sympathetically considered by the Fund, if so requested by the member concerned in accordance with the following formula:

Quotas below $5 million could be raised to $7.5 million;
Quotas of $5 million and above but below $10 million could be raised to $10 million;

[171] See below p. 66.
[172] In 1959 four Resolutions on quota increases were adopted by the Board of Governors of the Fund as follows: Resolution No. 14-1 relating to a General Increase by 50 per cent in the quotas in effect on January 31, 1959; Resolution No. 14-2 relating to increases in small quotas—under this Resolution the quotas of all members to which "the small quota policy of the Second Quinquennial Review" applies, may be increased to an amount not exceeding 50 per cent of the maximum quota available to them under this policy; Resolution No. 14-3 relating to special increases in the quotas of Canada, Federal Republic of Germany, and Japan. The Board of Governors adopted these Resolutions, effective February 2, 1959. For text, see IMF, *Summary Proceedings, 1959*, pp. 158-162. On April 6, 1959, the Board of Governors adopted a further Resolution (No. 14-4), under which fourteen members which had submitted special requests for quota increases could, subject to consent by September 15, 1959 and payment of the subscription by October 15, 1959, have their quotas increased to the amounts listed in the Resolution. For text, see IMF, *Summary Proceedings, 1959*, p. 161. Effective March 31, 1965, the Board of Governors adopted Resolutions No. 20-6 and 20-7. The First Resolution proposed that the quotas of all members be increased by 25 per cent. Under the Second Resolution special quota increases were proposed for 16 countries enumerated in the Resolution. For text, see IMF, *Summary Proceedings, 1965*, pp. 245-249.

Quotas of $10 million and above but below $15 million could be raised to $15 million; and

Quotas of $15 million and above but below $20 million could be raised to $20 million.

Similarly, Executive Board decision No. 1477-(63/8) of February 27, 1963, paragraph 3, provides that the Fund is willing to give sympathetic consideration to requests for the adjustments of the quotas of certain "primary exporting countries" with relatively small quotas, if such adjustment would make these quotas more adequate in the light of fluctuations in export proceeds and other relevant criteria.[173]

Apart from the above mentioned techniques of adjustment of quotas that affected more than one member, also individual quotas have been adjusted over the years in accordance with the second sentence of Article III, Section 2.

Changes in the quotas of members of the Fund are recorded by the Fund in several of its publications and the actual status of quotas is reported monthly in *International Financial Statistics*.

## 2. FUND RIGHTS AND RESPONSIBILITIES DERIVED FROM SOURCES OTHER THAN THE FUND AGREEMENT

There are at least two legal sources other than the Fund Agreement[174] from which rights and responsibilities of the Fund are derived: the General Agreement on Tariffs and Trade (GATT), concluded in 1947, and the General Arrangements to Borrow (GAB), concluded in 1962.

### (a) *General Agreement on Tariffs and Trade*

Under Article XV of GATT, the Contracting Parties to GATT, acting jointly, shall seek cooperation with the Fund so that both may pursue a coordinated policy with regard to exchange questions within the jurisdiction of the Fund and questions of quantitative restrictions

[173] For text of the Resolution, see IMF, *Selected Decisions*, pp. 40-43. For a list of countries whose quota was adjusted under this provision, see, IMF, *Annual Report, 1966*, p. 125 and IMF, *Annual Report, 1968*, p. 98.

[174] On the Agreement between the United Nations and the IMF, and on the Convention on the Privileges and Immunities of the Specialized Agencies, see Aufricht, *The International Monetary Fund*, pp. 16-18. On the Agreement between the IMF and Switzerland of June 11, 1964, see Joseph Gold, "The Fund and Non-Member States," IMF, Pamphlet Series No. 7 (Washington: 1966), pp. 33-37.

and other trade measures within the jurisdiction of the Contracting Parties.

Any detailed discussion of the complex provisions of GATT relating to trade measures is outside the scope of this study. Nevertheless, Article XV, paragraph 2, of GATT requires special mention, since it enumerates the principal powers which the Fund may exercise in its relations with the Contracting Parties and sets forth obligations of the Contracting Parties towards the Fund.

Under this provision, the Contracting Parties shall consult with the Fund whenever they have to deal with problems concerning monetary reserves, balances of payments, or foreign-exchange arrangements. In such consultations, the Contracting Parties shall accept all findings of statistical and other facts presented by the Fund relating to foreign exchange, monetary reserves, and balances of payments, and shall accept the determination of the Fund as to whether action by a contracting party in exchange matters is in accordance with the Fund Agreement or with the terms of a special exchange agreement between a contracting party and the Contracting Parties. Finally, the Contracting Parties shall in certain decisions under GATT accept the determination of the Fund as to what constitutes a serious decline in a contracting party's monetary reserves, a very low level of its monetary reserves, and on financial aspects of other matters covered in consultations in such cases.[175] In accordance with Article XV, paragraph 3 of GATT, the Fund and the Contracting Parties have concluded informal agreements regarding consultation and cooperation.[176]

(b) *General Arrangements to Borrow*

Special rights and obligations of the Fund are also derived from Borrowing Arrangements which entered into force on October 24, 1962.[177] These arrangements are embodied in two documents: one en-

[175] The original version of Art. XV, para. 2 refers only to decisions of the Contracting Parties involving the criteria set forth in para. 2(a) of Art. XII. The revised version also refers to decisions of the Contracting Parties involving the criteria set forth in para. 9 of Art. XVIII. On the relationship between the Fund and GATT, see also Ervin Hexner, "The General Agreement on Tariffs and Trade and the Monetary Fund," IMF, *Staff Papers*, vol. I (April 1951) pp. 432-464.

[176] For text of Exchange of Letters between the Fund and the Contracting Parties to GATT (1948), see IMF, *Annual Report, 1949*, pp. 75-78. On GATT-Fund relations, see also GATT doc. L/533, October 3, 1956, and SR 11/3, October 20, 1956, p. 18.

[177] On October 15, 1965 the Executive Directors approved renewal of the GAB for a period of four years from October 1966.

titled "General Arrangements to Borrow" (GAB), Executive Board Decision No. 1289-(62/1) of January 5, 1962 (hereafter referred to as "the Decision"),[178] and the other a letter (hereafter referred to as "the Letter") the text of which was exchanged among the ten participants (United States, the Deutsche Bundesbank [the central bank of Germany], United Kingdom, France, Italy, Japan, Canada, Netherlands, Belgium, and the Sveriges Riksbank [the central bank of Sweden]) in the arrangements.[179]

The Fund is not deemed to be a party to the Letter. However, the participants regard the Letter as an integral part of the Borrowing Arrangements.[180]

Under the GAB, the ten participants stand ready, subject to the terms and conditions of these arrangements, to lend their currencies to the Fund, up to amounts specified in the Annex, when supplementary resources are needed to forestall or cope with an impairment of the international monetary system. The total amounts available under the arrangements equal U.S. $6 billion.[181]

One of the principal considerations for arriving at these arrangements was, in the words of the Preamble to the Decision, to enable the Fund "to fulfil more effectively its role in the international monetary system in the new conditions of widespread convertibility, including greater freedom for short-term capital movements." Actually, the basic purpose of the GAB was to ensure a contingent commitment of the main industrial nations with balance-of-payments surpluses to make loans to

[178] For text of the Decision, see IMF, *Selected Decisions*, pp. 56-66.

[179] *Ibid.*, pp. 67-68. The Deutsche Bundesbank was deemed to be empowered under German Law to be a participant in the GAB. Hence no special legislative measure or authorization by the Legislature was required for Germany's participation in the credit arrangements under the GAB in an amount up to DM4 billion. In Sweden the Sveriges Riksbank was expressly empowered to grant credits to the IMF under the amended version of Art. 15 of the Sveriges Riksbank Act, 1934.

[180] The first paragraph of the Letter reads: "The purpose of this Letter is to set forth the understandings reached during the recent discussions in Paris with respect to the procedure to be followed by the Participating Countries and Institutions (hereinafter referred to as 'the participants') in connection with borrowings by the International Monetary Fund of Supplementary Resources under credit arrangements which we expect will be established pursuant to a decision of the Executive Directors of the Fund." IMF, *Selected Decisions*, p. 67.

[181] The maximum amounts of loanable funds under the contemplated credit arrangements pursuant to the GAB, expressed in millions of U.S. dollars, are as follows: Belgium 150; Canada 200; France 550; Deutsche Bundesbank 1,000; Italy 550; Japan 250; Netherlands 200; Sveriges Riksbank 100; United Kingdom 1,000; United States 2,000.

the Fund which, in turn, was expected to "lend" the proceeds of such loans to participants in the GAB whose balance-of-payments positions were impaired, primarily as a result of short-term capital outflows. Moreover, it was expected that the GAB would deter speculation against the currency of a country suffering from outflows of short-term capital.[182]

An increase of the Fund's resources by means of activation of the GAB is the result of a "loan" by the participants in the GAB. It therefore must be repaid by the Fund to the lender or lenders. Pending repayment, the GAB creditor has a claim against the Fund.[183] The rules governing repayment by the Fund to GAB creditors and those governing repurchase obligations of a member that has purchased currency from the Fund are regulated in considerable detail in paragraph 11 of the Decision.

Certain other features of the GAB are of special legal significance: (1) Unlike other formal decisions of the Executive Directors, whether or not they are taken under Article XVIII of the Fund Agreement, the Decision is not directly binding upon members. (2) Drawings by participants in the GAB are subject to special conditions;[184] there is no automatic or virtually automatic right of a member to purchase from the Fund "borrowed currency," that is, currency transferred to the Fund's account under a credit arrangement with GAB creditors. (3) The provisions on voting procedure differ from those normally applicable in the Fund.[185] Under the Letter (paragraph B) the participants shall, after consultation with the Managing Director of the Fund, aim at reaching a unanimous decision on the amounts of their currencies which they consider appropriate to lend to the Fund. If unanimity is reached among the potential lenders, no question of weighting the votes of individual lenders arises. In the absence of unanimity, a favorable decision on any request for a drawing requires

---

[182] On the climate of opinion in which the GAB was drafted—in particular, on the basic similarity of the proposals advanced by Xenophon Zolotas, E. M. Bernstein, and Per Jacobsson—see Fritz Machlup, *Plans for Reform of the International Monetary System*, Special Papers in International Economics, No. 3 (Princeton: International Finance Section, 1964), pp. 33-34.

[183] See, for example, IMF, *Annual Report, 1965*, p. 10.

[184] These conditions are set forth in paragraphs 6 and 7 of the Decision and in paragraphs A-D of the Letter.

[185] The normal voting procedure in the Fund is a combination of "weighted voting" with the majority principle. See, on this point, Art. XII, Sec. 5(a) and (d). As previously indicated (see above pp. 9-10), there are several exceptions to this procedure expressly provided in the Fund Agreement.

a two-thirds majority of the number of participants voting and a three-fifths majority of the weighted votes of the participants voting—that is, weighted on the basis of the commitments to furnish supplementary resources. The prospective drawer is expressly prohibited from voting in such majority decisions (paragraph C of the Letter). (4) Any question of interpretation raised in connection with the Decision which is not within the scope of Article XVIII of the Fund Agreement "shall be settled to the mutual satisfaction of the Fund, the participant raising the question, and all other participants." This formula means presumably that the interpretation of the Decision is not within the exclusive jurisdiction of the Fund, but that situations are envisaged in which the Fund, the participant raising the question, and all other participants will confer on an organ outside the Fund authority to interpret the Decision.

The GAB, originally designed to enable the Fund and the participants in the GAB to "forestall or cope with an impairment of the international monetary system," gave rise to another institutional arrangement, the "Group of Ten"—the ten members of the Fund participating in the GAB. In the period 1963-1967 the Group of Ten became, in consultation and cooperation with the Fund, the focal point for the study and evaluation of the principal proposals for reform of the international monetary system. In May 1965, the Deputies of the Ministers and Central Bank Governors of the Group of Ten released the *Report of the Study Group on the Creation of Reserve Assets* (or the Ossola Report) which, through lucid analysis of various proposals on the subject, contributed greatly to a clarification of the major relevant questions.

Following the 1966 Annual Meeting of the Board of Governors of the Fund, arrangements were made for informal meetings between the Executive Directors of the Fund and the Deputies. These joint deliberations led to the formulation and adoption by the Executive Directors and the Board of Governors of the *Outline of a Facility Based on Special Drawing Rights in the International Monetary Fund.*[186]

[186] For a lucid presentation of the economic and political implications of the Special Drawing Rights proposal, see Fritz Machlup, *Remaking the International Monetary System: The Rio Agreement and Beyond* (Baltimore: Johns Hopkins Press, 1968). For a discussion of whether SDR's are to be considered as assets, credit or money, see especially pp. 38-39, 90-92, and 92-93. Machlup interprets the term "Special Drawing Rights" by reference to the *travaux préparatoires* as follows: "The Report of the Deputies of the Group of Ten, submitted to the

## 3. The Agreement on Special Drawing Rights

A major change in the functions of the Fund is now envisaged in the proposed amendments to the Fund Agreement relating to Special Drawing Rights. These amendments have been formulated by the Executive Directors of the Fund in a new Introductory Article and in additions to the original Articles of Agreement set forth in Articles XXI through XXXII and Schedules F, G, H and I.[187]

These amendments, together with an explanatory note, have been presented for the first time in "A Report by the Executive Directors to the Board of Governors Proposing Amendment of the Articles of Agreement," which was released by the Fund on April 16, 1968. The Report of the Executive Directors was approved by the Board of Governors on May 31, 1968. The Amendment to take effect will have to be accepted by three-fifths of all the members, provided the accepting members account for four-fifths of the total voting power. In addition, members having 75 per cent of total quotas are required to deposit instruments of participation in the Special Drawing Account before it can become operational (Article XVII and Article XXIII, Section 1).

---

Ministers and Governors in July 1966, distinguished two alternative approaches to the creation of new reserve assets: 'The two basic forms of reserve asset that we have considered are drawing rights and reserve units.' The chief difference was that drawing rights were seen as rights against the Fund, to draw convertible currencies from the IMF (or another agency), whereas reserve units were claims transferable directly among participants. . . . Evidently, the quick change in the word meanings was a matter of diplomatic convenience. The term 'reserve unit' had become unacceptable to one government. By calling the new reserve asset 'drawing right,' although it was no longer a right to draw currencies from the Fund and although it was made directly transferable among participants, it became possible to agree on its creation. If this terminological flexibility is understood, there should be no difficulty in comprehending the character of the special drawing rights adopted by the Rio Agreement." *Ibid.*, pp. 77-78. For text of the Outline, see IMF, *Summary Proceedings, 1967*, pp. 272-279. For comments on the Outline, see also E. M. Bernstein, "The Contingency Plan for a New Reserve Facility," in Model, Roland & Co. *Quarterly Review and Investment Survey* (Fourth Quarter 1967), pp. 1-12; Joseph Gold, "The Next Stage in the Development of International Monetary Law: the Deliberate Control of Liquidity," *American Journal of International Law*, vol. 62 (April 1968), pp. 365-402; and James R. Atwood, John H. Barton, Nolan E. Clark, "Legal Problems of International Monetary Reform," *Stanford Law Review*, vol. 20 (May 1968), pp. 870-999.

[187] For text of the proposed Amendment, see *April 1968 Report of the Executive Directors* (cited in footnote 3), pp. 36-73. The IMF also published in 1968 a document entitled *Articles of Agreement of the International Monetary Fund as modified by the proposed Amendment* to indicate the changes in the text of the 1944 version of the Fund Agreement that would result from adoption of the proposed Amendment.

(a) *General Account and Special Drawing Account*

Under the provisions proposed, the Fund shall maintain a General Account and a Special Drawing Account [Introductory Article (ii)]. Transactions and operations involving Special Drawing Rights shall be conducted through the Special Drawing Account, while other transactions between members and the Fund, such as subscriptions by members, adjustments of quotas, direct purchases by a member of the currency of another member, shall be recorded in the General Account [Introductory Article (iii)].

Normally SDR's will be held by the participating members but, under Article XXIII, Section 2, the Fund itself is empowered to accept and hold SDR's in the General Account and to use them in accordance with the provisions of the Fund Agreement; operations and transactions pursuant to this provision shall be conducted through the General Account as well as the Special Drawing Account (Article XXII, Section 1).

(b) *Participants*

A member of the Fund is entitled to participate in the Special Drawing Account [Introductory Article (ii)] provided the member deposits with the Fund an Instrument of Participation stating that the member undertakes all the obligations of a participant in the Special Drawing Account in accordance with its law and that it has taken all steps necessary to enable it to carry out these obligations (Article XXIII, Section 1).

(c) *Allocation and Cancellation of Special Drawing Rights*

The Fund is empowered to allocate SDR's to participants in the Special Drawing Account to meet the need, as and when it arises, for a supplement to existing reserve assets (Article XXI, Section 1).

Any decision to allocate SDR's will (1) determine the *basic period*, normally five years, and (2) the *rate of allocation* expressed in terms of a specified percentage, uniform for all, of the quotas of the participants. Any allocation of SDR's shall take place at yearly intervals [Article XXIV, Section 2(a) and (b)]. To illustrate: Assuming that the basic period is five years and the percentage rate of allocation is fixed at 10 per cent of quota, the maximum Special Drawing Rights on the basis of present quotas in the Fund would amount to $516 million for the United States, $244 million for the United Kingdom and $120 million for the Federal Republic of Germany.[188]

If there are unexpected major developments, the Fund may (1) change the rate of allocation or the interval of allocation during the rest of the basic period, or (2) change the length of the basic period, or (3) start a new basic period (Article XXIV, Section 3).

Decisions on allocation of SDR's are not irrevocable. Actually, the Fund is expressly empowered to cancel SDR's. Cancellation of these rights, like allocations, shall also be made for basic periods which shall run consecutively and shall normally be five years in duration [Article XXIV, Section 2(a)].[189]

(d) *Principles Governing Allocation of Special Drawing Rights*

In its decisions on the allocation of SDR's the Fund shall seek to meet the long-term global need to supplement existing reserve assets in a manner which will promote the purposes of the Fund and will avoid economic stagnation and deflation as well as excess demand or inflation [Article XXIV, Section 1(a)].

The same principles shall also govern decisions of the Fund to cancel SDR's [Article XXIV, Section 1(a)].

The first decision to allocate SDR's shall also take into account certain special considerations. The first of these special considerations is a "collective judgment" that there is a global need to supplement reserves. The term "collective judgment" is designed to reflect the requirement of an 85 per cent majority of the total voting power for the adoption by the Board of Governors of decisions to allocate SDR's. Other special considerations are the attainment of a better balance-of-payments equilibrium and the likelihood of a better working of the adjustment process in the future [Article XXIV, Section 1(b)].

(e) *Receipt of Allocation*

Article XXIV, Section 2(e) specifies that a participant shall receive allocations of SDR's, meaning that he is required to accept such allo-

[188] On the "Impact of hypothetical Allocation of SDR's on the Balances of Payments of Fund Member Countries," see Machlup, *Remaking the International Monetary System, op.cit.,* Appendix E, pp. 152-155.

[189] Notwithstanding the provisions of Art. XXIV, Sec. 2(a) and (b), the Fund may decide, by virtue of Art. XXIV, Sec. 2(c), that the duration of the basic period shall be other than five years; the allocations or cancellation shall take place at other than yearly intervals; the basis for allocation or cancellation shall be the quotas on dates other than the dates of decisions to allocate or cancel Special Drawing Rights.

cations. However, the Article also provides that the participant does not have to accept such allocations (1) if the Governor voting for the participant did not vote in favor of the decision to allocate SDR's; or (2) if the participant prior to the first allocation of SDR's, has notified the Fund in writing that it does not wish SDR's to be allocated to it. In other words, even a member that has deposited an Instrument of Participation in respect of the Special Drawing Account in accordance with Article XXIII, Section 1, may "opt out" of the provision under which it must accept allocation of SDR's.

On the request of a participant, the Fund may decide to terminate the effect of a notification of that participant that it does not wish SDR's to be allocated to it. As soon as the Fund's decision on such a request takes effect the participant is required to accept SDR's.

### (f) Use of Special Drawing Rights

Under Article XXV, Section 2(a) a participant is entitled to use its Special Drawing Rights to obtain an equivalent amount of currency from a participant designated by the Fund pursuant to Article XXV, Section 5. A participant that provides currency to a participant using SDR's shall receive an equivalent amount of SDR's [Article XXV, Section 2(c)].

There is a limit on the amount a participant may use; a participant is generally expected to carry over a five-year period a minimum balance of 30 per cent of the allocation of SDR's it has received [Schedule G(a)(i)].

In agreement with another participant, a participant may use its SDR's also to obtain an equivalent amount of its own currency held by the other participant [Article XXV, Section 2(b)(i)] and for other transactions specified in Article XXV, Section 2(b)(ii).

Interest, charges, and assessments in regard of SDR's as they become due under Article XXVI, Sections 1-4 shall be "paid" in SDR's (Article XXVI, Section 5).[190] Also, the Fund shall accept SDR's in repurchases accruing in these rights under the amended version of Article V, Section 7(b).[191]

[190] See also Art. XXII, Sec. 2, which provides that the Fund shall be reimbursed periodically for the expenses of administering the Special Drawing Account from the resources held in the General Account. For the purpose of such reimbursement, the Fund will levy assessments under Art. XXVI, Sec. 4 on all participants in proportion to their net cumulative allocations. The amounts assessed are payable in Special Drawing Rights directly into the General Account.
[191] See also Art. XXV, Sec. 7(b)(i).

A participant designated by the Fund under Article XXV, Section 5 shall provide on demand currency convertible in fact[192] to a participant using SDR's under Article XXV, Section 2(a) (Article XXV, Section 4).

No participant is obliged to hold more than three times its net cumulative allocation. Thus, if a participant has been allocated $100 million worth of SDR's, it must accept another $200 million from member countries in weaker reserve position; it may agree to take even more (Article XXV, Section 4).

In transactions between participants a participant may need to use its SDR's to meet balance-of-payments deficits or to counteract certain developments in its official holdings of gold, foreign exchange, and SDR's or in its reserve position in the Fund due to conversion of its currency. While such use of its SDR's may change the composition of the member's reserve assets, the member is expected not to use its SDR's for the sole purpose of such change [Article XXV, Section 3(a)].

The use of SDR's shall not be subject to challenge by the Fund that the participant does not meet the expectation of Article XXV, Section 3(a), but the Fund may make representation to a participant that fails to fulfil this expectation. If a participant persists in failing to fulfil this expectation, the Fund may suspend the right of that participant to use SDR's [Article XXV, Section 3(b) and Article XXIX, Section 2(b)].

## (g) *Who Shall Supply Currency?*

The Fund shall ensure that a participant will be able to use its SDR's by designating participants to provide currency for specified amounts of SDR's for the purposes of Sections 2(a) and 4 of Article XXV [Article XXV, Section 5(a)].

A participant shall generally be "subject to designation" if its balance of payments and gross reserve position are sufficiently strong; however, a participant may be designated by the Fund even though it has a moderate balance-of-payments deficit, if its reserve position is strong. Participants shall be designated in such manner as will promote over time a balanced distribution of drawing rights among them [Article XXV, Section 5 (a)(i); see also Schedule F].

[192] For definition of "currency convertible in fact," see Art. XXXII(b).

## (h) Reconstitution

Participants that use their Special Drawing Rights shall reconstitute their holdings of these rights in accordance with the rules for reconstitution in Schedule G, unless other rules for reconstitution have been adopted, at the end of the first or each subsequent basic period. An 85 per cent majority of total voting power shall be required for decisions to adopt, modify, or abrogate the rules for reconstitution (Article XXV, Section 6).[193]

Schedule G sets forth the rules for reconstitution applicable during the first basic period; it provides, in particular, that a participant shall so use and reconstitute its holdings of SDR's that—five years after the first allocation and at the end of each calendar quarter thereafter—the average of its daily holdings of SDR's over the most recent five-year period will be not less than 30 per cent of the average of daily net cumulative allocation[194] of SDR's over the same period.

If a participant needs to acquire SDR's to comply with this obligation and if a participant is unable to obtain sufficient drawing rights from another designated participant, it shall acquire SDR's through the Fund's General Account for gold or currency acceptable to the Fund or from another participant specified by the Fund to the extent that the General Account is unable to supply them [Schedule G(1)(a) (iv)].

If a participant fails to comply with these rules for reconstitution, the Fund shall determine whether or not circumstances justify suspension of the right to use SDR's under Article XXIX, Section 2(b).

## (j) Interest and Charges

Under Article XXVI, Sections 1 and 2, interest shall be credited and interest charged, respectively, on the holdings by participants of SDR's and on their net cumulative allocation of SDR's. In actual practice, these provisions will result in the payment of interest by the Fund to a participant on the excess of its holdings of SDR's over its net cumulative allocations, and in the payment of charges by a par-

[193] On the rule of reconstitution of balances, see Machlup, *Remaking the International Monetary System, op.cit.,* pp. 54 and 87-88.

[194] Art. XXXII(a) provides: "Net cumulative allocation of special drawing rights means the total amount of special drawing rights allocated to a participant less its share of special drawing rights that have been cancelled under Article XXIV, Section 2(a)."

ticipant on the amount by which its holdings of SDR's are less than its net cumulative allocation.

The rate of interest shall be the same as the rate of charges. Under Article XXVI, Section 3, this rate is determined at 1½ per cent per annum, but the Fund is authorized to raise this rate up to 2 per cent or to the same level as the remuneration to be paid to members under Article V, Section 9.

Interest and charges are payable in SDR's (Article XXVI, Section 5).

### 4. Modifications of the Original Articles of Agreement

Heretofore all changes in the living law of the Fund have resulted *directly* from interpretative decisions of the Executive Board or practical construction of the Fund Agreement by various organs of the Fund, or *indirectly* from specific provisions of international agreements, such as Article XV of GATT, that confer rights and responsibilities on the Fund.

The April 1968 Report by the Executive Directors proposed for the first time a formal amendment to the Fund Agreement under Article XVII of that Agreement. Proposed modifications of the original Articles of Agreement were published by the Fund on pp. 36-44 of the April 1968 Report of the Executive Directors; these modifications affect Articles I, III, IV, V, VI, XII, XVIII, XIX, XX and Schedule B.[195]

### (a) Majority decisions

One group of amendments changes the majorities required for certain Fund decisions.

Changes in quotas that result from a general review of quotas will require 85 per cent of the total voting power; however, an 80 per cent majority of the total voting power is prescribed for decisions on any other change in quotas (Article III, Section 2).

An 85 per cent majority is also required for decisions on the question of whether a member will be permitted in the event of a quota increase to pay less than 25 per cent of its additional subscription in gold [Article III, Section 4(c)].

For decisions on a uniform proportionate change of par values an 85 per cent majority is called for; by contrast the original Articles of

[195] For comment, see Fritz Machlup, *Remaking the International Monetary System, op.cit.*, pp. 132-133 and A.G.B. Fisher, "The International Monetary Fund: Act II," *The Banker* (November 1968), pp. 259-263.

Agreement provide for a simple majority and the approval by those members that have 10 per cent or more of the total of the quotas (Article IV, Section 7).[196]

An 85 per cent majority is also required for a waiver of the maintenance of the gold value of the Fund's assets in the event of a uniform proportionate change of par values [Article IV, Section 8(d)].

Decisions requiring an 85 per cent majority under the proposed Amendment, whether with respect to the General Account or the Special Drawing Account, are to be taken by the Board of Governors [Article XII, Section 2(b) and Article XXIV, Section 4(a) and (d)].

(b) *Fund Transactions, Charges, and Remuneration*

In Article I(v) and in the new subsection (c) of Section 3 of Article V express reference is made to the principle that use of the Fund's resources in the General Account shall be temporary.[197]

Under the proposed Amendment the term "gold-tranche purchase," which is not used in the original Articles of Agreement, will be incorporated in the text of the Fund Agreement for the first time; it will appear in Article V, Section 3(a)(iii), Article V, Section 3(d) and Article V, Section 8(a). The proposed new version of Article VI, Section 2 authorizes a member to make gold-tranche purchases to meet capital transfers.[198]

The provisions on repurchase by a member of its currency held by the Fund will be modified by amendments of Article V, Section 7(b) and (c), inclusion of a new subsection (d) under Section 7, and amendment of Schedule B. As previously mentioned, the Fund will accept Special Drawing Rights in repurchases under Article V, Section 7(b) [Article XXV, Section 7(b)(i)].[199]

The Articles as amended will permit the Fund to reduce or eliminate the service charge (presently at ½ per cent) on gold-tranche purchases [Article V, Section 8(a)].

The proposed Amendment also provides for the payment of a remuneration on the Fund's net use of the currency subscription of

[196] See above p. 10.

[197] Art. V, Sec. 3(c) provides: "The Fund shall adopt policies on the use of its resources that will assist members to solve their balance of payments problems in a manner consistent with the purposes of the Fund and that will establish adequate safeguards for the temporary use of its resources."

[198] For definition of "gold-tranche purchase," see below p. 69.

[199] For a detailed discussion of the proposed change in the rules on repurchases, see *April 1968 Report of the Executive Directors*, pp. 25-28.

a member. The remuneration will be payable "on the amount by which seventy-five percent of a member's quota exceeded the average of the Fund's holdings of the member's currency, provided that no account shall be taken of holdings in excess of seventy-five percent of quota" (Article V, Section 9).[200]

The remuneration shall be paid in gold or in the currency of the member which is entitled to the remuneration as determined by the Fund (Article V, Section 9).

### (c) Interpretation

As previously mentioned, under Article XVIII(a) of the Fund Agreement any question of interpretation of the Agreement between any member and the Fund or between any members of the Fund shall be submitted to the Executive Directors for their decision.[201] Under the original Articles of Agreement any member may require that such an interpretative decision be referred to the Board of Governors, whose decision shall be final [Article XVIII(b)]. No request for review by the Board of Governors of an interpretative decision by the Executive Directors has been made since the inception of the Fund's activities in May 1946.

The proposed amendment to Article XVIII provides that any request by a member for review by the Board of Governors of a decision of the Executive Directors must be made within three months from the date of that decision. Moreover, any question referred to the Board of Governors shall be considered by a Committee of the Board of Governors. Each Committee member shall have one vote. The Board of Governors shall prescribe the membership, procedures, and voting majorities of the Committee. The decision of the Committee shall be the decision of the Board of Governors, *unless* the Board by an 85 per cent majority of the total voting power decides otherwise.

The voting procedure in the Committee to be established is an exception to the principle of weighted voting set forth in Article XII, Section 5(a): "Each member shall have two hundred fifty votes plus one additional vote for each part of its quota equivalent to one hundred thousand United States dollars." While under the original Articles of Agreement a simple majority of the Board of Governors

---

[200] The IMF, *Annual Report, 1968*, p. 16, refers in this context to the super-gold-tranche position when it states: "The Proposed Amendment also provides for the payment of remuneration to members that hold what has become known as a super gold tranche position in the Fund."

[201] See above p. 15.

was prescribed for interpretative decisions of that Board,[202] a majority of 85 per cent of the total voting power will be required for a decision by the Board of Governors *to review* a decision of the Committee. Nevertheless, Article XVIII(b) as amended permits the conclusion that a decision of the Board of Governors on the merits of a question referred to it for decision may be arrived at by a simple majority of the total voting power.

(d) *Definitions*

Through modification of Article XIX(a) and (e) a gross concept of monetary reserves has replaced the net concept of reserves as the basis of the computation of members' repurchase obligations and for other purposes.

Under Article XIX(j) a "gold-tranche purchase" means a purchase by a member of the currency of another member in exchange for its own currency which does not cause the Fund's holdings of the member's currency to exceed 100 per cent of its quota; however, the Fund may exclude from this definition purchases and holdings under policies on the use of its resources for compensatory financing of export fluctuations.

For participants in the Special Drawing Account a participant's "reserve position in the Fund" means the sum of the gold-tranche purchases it could make and the amount of any indebtedness of the Fund that is readily repayable to the participant under a loan agreement [Article XXXII(c)].

[202] The requirement of a simple majority vote may be inferred from Art. XII, Sec. 5(d) of the Fund Agreement, which reads: "Except as otherwise specifically provided, all decisions of the Fund shall be made by a majority of the votes cast."

69

## VI. RETROSPECT AND PROSPECT

### 1. Past Trends

In Chapter III of this study the legal framework of drawing rights in the Fund was expounded. At the same time major changes in the Fund's lending policies in the period 1947-1968 were traced by reference to relevant decisions of the Executive Directors of the Fund. It was shown, in particular, that as a matter of law all drawing rights in the Fund were conditional[203]—that is to say, members may exercise them only in the contingencies defined in the provisions of the Fund Agreement governing the exercise of drawing rights[204] in the Fund.

Moreover, the Fund Agreement confers on the Fund discretionary powers in respect of the following matters: (1) Under Article V, Section 4, the Fund may on terms which safeguard its interests waive any of the conditions prescribed in Article V, Section 3(a) of the Fund Agreement. (2) The Fund may postpone exchange transactions with any member if its circumstances are such that, in the opinion of the Fund, such transactions would lead to use of the resources of the Fund in a manner contrary to the purposes of the Fund Agreement [Article XX, Section 4(i)].[205] (3) The Fund may make a finding that a member is using the resources of the Fund in a manner incompatible with the purposes of the Fund (Article V, Section 5). (4) The Fund may declare a member ineligible to use the Fund's resources; such declaration of ineligibility to engage in direct purchases may be based on the provisions of Article V, Section 5 (relating to use of the Fund's resources contrary to the purposes of the Fund); or on Article VI, Section 1 (relating to use of the Fund's resources to meet a large or sustained outflow of capital); or on Article XV, Section 2(a) (authorizing the Fund to declare ineligible any member that

---

[203] See, however, the *April 1968 Report of the Executive Directors*, which states on p. 23: "One of the effects of the modifications in Article V, Section 3, will be to make the use of the Fund's resources in the gold tranche legally automatic." For a critical discussion of this statement, see below pp. 72-73.

[204] The term "drawing right" or "drawing rights" is *not* used in the Fund Agreement; but it is a convenient shorthand expression for the technically more precise, but rather cumbersome phrase used in Art. V, Sec. 3(a) of the Fund Agreement, which reads: "A member shall be entitled to buy the currency of another member from the Fund in exchange for its own currency . . ."

[205] On the interpretation of Art. XX, Sec. 4(i) by Executive Board Decision No. 284-2 of March 10, 1948, see above p. 22.

fails to fulfil any of its obligations under the Fund Agreement).[206]

Up to now, the Fund has exercised the discretionary powers conferred upon it by the foregoing provisions only in connection with the application of Article V, Section 4 (relating to waiver of conditions). It would probably be erroneous to infer that the discretionary powers vested in the Fund by virtue of the above-mentioned other provisions of the Fund Agreement have lapsed on the ground that these provisions have never been invoked by the Fund in the period 1947 to 1968. On the contrary, a more persuasive view holds the above-mentioned discretionary powers constitute residual rights on which the Fund may rely in appropriate circumstances. One possible interpretation of the frequently used phrase that in respect of specified transactions a member has "virtually automatic" access to the Fund's resources would be that the Fund, notwithstanding its generally liberal or lenient attitude toward specified categories of drawing rights, has retained its power to invoke one or all of the above-mentioned residual rights for the purpose of postponing, if necessary indefinitely, a transaction with a member that *otherwise* would enjoy automatic access to the Fund's resources.

## 2. Future Lending Policies

At this juncture the question may be raised of the probable effect which the new facility of Special Drawing Rights and the proposed Amendment of the first twenty Articles of the Fund Agreement may have upon the Fund's lending policies. In particular, it may be asked which of the following alternatives are envisaged in the proposed Amendment and in the related comments contained in the April 1968 report of the Executive Directors: (1) Will the lending policies of the Fund be further liberalized by extending the scope of virtually automatic access to the Fund's resources beyond the categories of transactions that were specified by September 1968? (2) Will the scope of virtual automaticity of traditional drawing rights under the Fund Agreement attained by September 1968 be retained? (3) Will some of the lending policies that have been proclaimed through September 1968 subsequently be discontinued and give way to more stringent

[206] Art. V, Sec. 3(iv) cites Art. IV, Sec. 6 of the Fund Agreement as if it were one of the provisions under which the Fund may declare a member ineligible to use the resources of the Fund. Actually, under Art. IV, Sec. 6, a member that changes the par value of its currency despite the objection of the Fund becomes *ipso facto* ineligible to use the resources of the Fund, unless the Fund otherwise determines.

guidelines on the use of the Fund's resources at the time the Special Drawing Rights become available?

There is one passage in the April 1968 report of the Executive Directors which at first glance suggests that the second alternative has been aimed at; it reads: ". . . while one of the effects of these modifications will be to prevent the establishment of new facilities for unconditional use of the Fund's resources, they are not intended to make the rules and practices relating to the use of the Fund's resources more restrictive than they are at the present time."[207]

Upon closer examination it appears, however, that this statement is not free from ambiguity, for the following reasons: First, the statement seems to assume that the gold-tranche policy, prior to the entry into force of the proposed Amendment, permits unconditional rather than virtually automatic use of the Fund's resources. Second, it may be argued that, although the proposed modifications are at present not intended to make the rules and practices relating to the use of the Fund's resources more restrictive, these modifications do not prevent the Fund from deciding in the future that certain policies on the use of the Fund's resources, for example, the guidelines on "Compensatory Financing of Export Fluctuations" will be modified in a manner that will make them more restrictive than they are at present.

As regards "legal automaticity of gold-tranche purchases" or "unconditional use of the Fund's resources" the following passage from the *April 1968 Report of the Executive Directors* (p. 23) may be noted:

> Requests for gold tranche purchases now enjoy *de facto* automaticity. One of the effects of the modifications in Article V, Section 3, will be to make the use of the Fund's resources in the gold tranche legally automatic.
>
> After the amendment, the use of the Fund's resources in the gold tranche will continue to be subject to the provisions of Article V, Section 3(a). Accordingly, members making requests for purchases in the gold tranche will still be required to make the representation of need prescribed by Article V, Section 3(a)(i). However, the Fund will not have the legal power to challenge this representation.

It is questionable whether it is correct to say that requests for gold-tranche purchases now enjoy *de facto* automaticity. As previously

[207] *April 1968 Report of the Executive Directors*, pp. 20-21.

stated, it is preferable to speak of "virtual automaticity" on the ground that under Article XX, Section 4(i) of the Fund Agreement the Fund may postpone exchange transactions, including gold-tranche purchases, with any member if its circumstances are such that, in the opinion of the Fund, they would lead to use of the Fund's resources in a manner that is contrary to the purposes of the Fund Agreement or prejudicial to the Fund or the members.

We should also note that under the proposed new Article V, Section 3(d), "gold tranche purchases shall not be subject to challenge" or, in the words of the Executive Directors, "the Fund will not have the legal power to challenge"[208] the representation of need prescribed by Article V, Section 3(a)(i). Only on the assumption that the power to challenge the representation is the *only* basis on which the use of the Fund's resources could be denied would it be persuasive to say that the repeal of this power by the new Article V, Section 3(d) will "make the use of the Fund's resources in the gold tranche legally automatic."[209]

Most important, however, to note here is the fact that the proposed Amendment changes the title of Article XX of the Fund Agreement from "Final Provisions" to "Inaugural Provisions." This change may be merely a matter of style, necessitated by the fact that, as a result of the proposed Amendment, Article XX will no longer be the final Article of the Fund Agreement. It is not altogether inconceivable, however, that some people might argue that the heading "Inaugural Provisions" purports to affect the substantive provisions of Article XX by conferring on them the character of transitional provisions which thereby might have lost their legal force as soon as the Fund was inaugurated in the period March to May 1946.[210]

---

[208] *Ibid.*, p. 23.

[209] *Ibid.*

[210] As against this conceivable argument, it is submitted that under general rules of interpretation a title or a marginal heading of a legal provision may be invoked as an aid in interpretation only on the condition (1) that the substance of the provision is unclear, and (2) that the marginal heading is clear and thus apt to clarify the implications of an otherwise unclear provision. It is this writer's strong conviction that in accordance with this general rule of interpretation the change of the heading of Article XX from "Final Provisions" to "Inaugural Provisions" can not legally modify any of the provisions of the Fund Agreement that are clear and of a permanent nature. In particular, Article XX, Section 4(i) of the original Articles of Agreement remains one of the essential safeguards against misuse of the Fund's resources.

## 3. Scope of the Fund's Activities

By July 1969, twenty-five years will have elapsed since the United Nations Monetary and Financial Conference met at Bretton Woods, New Hampshire, to agree on the Articles of Agreement of the International Monetary Fund and of the International Bank for Reconstruction and Development.

In the course of the Fund's history, its membership has increased from 22 on December 27, 1945 to 111 by September 1968. By February 1969, exchange transactions with members had reached a total of $17.3 billion. There is every indication that the provisions for Special Drawing Rights, which are expected to enter into force in the near future, will constitute a major and significant innovation in the field of international monetary and credit relations and that they will have a direct impact on the liquidity position of members.

The Fund's function to serve as a forum in the field of international monetary cooperation [Article I(1)] has been greatly enhanced over the years: in effect, this function has been discharged on various levels. The Board of Governors, especially during the Annual Meetings, and the Executive Board are the principal organs through which the Fund functions as a forum of collaboration on international monetary matters. Periodic or *ad hoc* consultations between the Fund and the members are normally carried out by staff teams; the previously mentioned periodic consultations under Article XIV and Article VIII between the staff of the Fund and representatives of members are subject to review by the Executive Board.

The Fund's staff, which by now comprises more than 1,000 persons, has from the outset been engaged in research, primarily in the fields of economics and law, in order to enable the Fund to discharge effectively its functions of advice to and consultations with members.

The Fund Agreement provides specifically that the Fund shall act as a center for the collection and exchange of information on monetary and financial problems, both as an end in itself and as a means of facilitating the formulation of policies which further the purposes of the Fund. Some of the results of these activities are made available to the public through publications such as the annual *Balance of Payments Yearbook* and the monthly *International Financial Statistics*. The Fund publishes furthermore a periodical, *Staff Papers*, and from time to time monographs on economics[211] or law.[212]

[211] *Surveys of African Economies*, vol. I. Cameroon, Central African Republic, Chad, Congo (Brazzaville), Gabon (Washington: IMF, 1968).
[212] Joseph Gold, *The Fund Agreement in the Courts* (Washington: IMF, 1962).

The Fund renders technical assistance to members primarily as regards central banking, fiscal affairs, and statistics. The technical-assistance activities of the Fund include assignment of individual staff members, or of experts selected by the Fund, for a specified period to the monetary or fiscal authorities of members, as well as *ad hoc* technical-assistance missions carried out by individual staff members or staff teams. The latter advise in such areas as central banking and monetary reforms, tax legislation and tax administration, or assist members in reorganizing or setting up services in one of the fields in which the Fund has developed special statistical techniques (monetary statistics, balance-of-payments statistics).

Beginning with 1951, the Fund has operated in Washington training programs for qualified nationals of members, mostly from the central-bank or government staffs of member countries.

Thus, the scope of the Fund's activities has constantly increased over the years and it is to be expected that this trend will persist in the foreseeable future.

# APPENDIX I

Status of Membership of the
INTERNATIONAL MONETARY FUND

(*111 Member Countries*)
(November 1, 1968)

| Government of | Date of Signature of Articles of Agreement | Date of Deposit of Instrument of Acceptance |
|---|---|---|
| Afghanistan | July 14, 1955 | July 14, 1955 |
| Algeria | Sept. 26, 1963 | Sept. 26, 1963 |
| Argentina | Sept. 20, 1956 | Sept. 20, 1956 |
| Australia | Aug. 5, 1947 | Aug. 5, 1947 |
| Austria | Aug. 27, 1948 | Aug. 27, 1948 |
| [1] Belgium | Dec. 27, 1945 | Dec. 27, 1945 |
| [1] Bolivia | Dec. 27, 1945 | Dec. 27, 1945 |
| Botswana | July 24, 1968 | July 24, 1968 |
| [1] Brazil | Dec. 27, 1945 | Jan. 14, 1946[3] |
| Burma | Jan. 3, 1952 | Jan. 3, 1952 |
| Burundi | Sept. 28, 1963 | Sept. 28, 1963 |
| Cameroon | July 10, 1963 | July 10, 1963 |
| [1] Canada | Dec. 27, 1945 | Dec. 27, 1945 |
| Central African Republic | July 10, 1963 | July 10, 1963 |
| Ceylon | Aug. 29, 1950 | Aug. 29, 1950 |
| Chad | July 10, 1963 | July 10, 1963 |
| [1] Chile | Dec. 31, 1945 | Dec. 31, 1945 |
| [1] China | Dec. 27, 1945[3] | Dec. 26, 1945 |
| [1] Colombia | Dec. 27, 1945 | Dec. 27, 1945 |
| Congo (Brazzaville) | July 10, 1963 | July 10, 1963 |
| Congo, Dem. Rep. of | Sept. 28, 1963 | Sept. 28, 1963 |
| [1] Costa Rica | Dec. 27, 1945 | Jan. 8, 1946[3] |
| [1, 4] (Cuba) | (Dec. 31, 1945) | (Mar. 14, 1946)[3] |
| Cyprus | Dec. 21, 1961 | Dec. 21, 1961 |
| [1, 4] (Czechoslovakia) | (Dec. 27, 1945)[3] | (Dec. 26, 1945) |
| Dahomey | July 10, 1963 | July 10, 1963 |
| [2] Denmark | Mar. 30, 1946 | Mar. 30, 1946 |
| [1] Dominican Republic | Dec. 28, 1945 | Dec. 28, 1945 |
| [1] Ecuador | Dec. 27, 1945 | Dec. 28, 1945[3] |
| [2] El Salvador | Mar. 14, 1946 | Mar. 14, 1946 |
| [1] Ethiopia | Dec. 27, 1945[3] | Dec. 12, 1945 |
| Finland | Jan. 14, 1948 | Jan. 14, 1948 |
| [1] France | Dec. 27, 1945 | Dec. 27, 1945 |
| Gabon | Sept. 10, 1963 | Sept. 10, 1963 |
| Gambia, The | Sept. 21, 1967 | Sept. 21, 1967 |
| Germany | Aug. 14, 1952 | Aug. 14, 1952 |
| Ghana | Sept. 20, 1957 | Sept. 20, 1957 |
| [1] Greece | Dec. 27, 1945[3] | Dec. 26, 1945 |

77

| Government of | Date of Signature of Articles of Agreement | Date of Deposit of Instrument of Acceptance |
|---|---|---|
| [1] Guatemala | Dec. 27, 1945 | Dec. 28, 1945[3] |
| Guinea | Sept. 28, 1963 | Sept. 28, 1963 |
| Guyana | Sept. 26, 1966 | Sept. 26, 1966 |
| Haiti | Sept. 8, 1953 | Sept. 8, 1953 |
| [1] Honduras | Dec. 27, 1945[3] | Dec. 26, 1945 |
| [1] Iceland | Dec. 27, 1945 | Dec. 27, 1945 |
| [1] India | Dec. 27, 1945 | Dec. 27, 1945 |
| [5] Indonesia | Feb. 21, 1967 | Feb. 21, 1967 |
| [1] Iran | Dec. 28, 1945 | Dec. 29, 1945[3] |
| [1] Iraq | Dec. 27, 1945[3] | Dec. 26, 1945 |
| Ireland | Aug. 8, 1957 | Aug. 8, 1957 |
| Israel | July 12, 1954 | July 12, 1954 |
| Italy | Mar. 27, 1947 | Mar. 27, 1947 |
| Ivory Coast | Mar. 11, 1963 | Mar. 11, 1963 |
| Jamaica | Feb. 21, 1963 | Feb. 21, 1963 |
| Japan | Aug. 13, 1952 | Aug. 13, 1952 |
| Jordan | Aug. 29, 1952 | Aug. 29, 1952 |
| Kenya | Feb. 3, 1964 | Feb. 3, 1964 |
| Korea | Aug. 26, 1955 | Aug. 26, 1955 |
| Kuwait | Sept. 13, 1962 | Sept. 13, 1962 |
| Laos | July 5, 1961 | July 5, 1961 |
| Lebanon | Apr. 14, 1947[3] | Apr. 11, 1947 |
| Lesotho | July 25, 1968 | July 25, 1968 |
| Liberia | Mar. 28, 1962 | Mar. 28, 1962 |
| Libya | Sept. 17, 1958 | Sept. 17, 1958 |
| [1] Luxembourg | Dec. 27, 1945[3] | Dec. 26, 1945 |
| Malagasy Republic | Sept. 25, 1963 | Sept. 25, 1963 |
| Malawi | July 19, 1965 | July 19, 1965 |
| Malaysia | Mar. 7, 1958 | Mar. 7, 1958 |
| Mali | Sept. 27, 1963 | Sept. 27, 1963 |
| Malta | Sept. 11, 1968 | Sept. 11, 1968 |
| Mauritania | Sept. 10, 1963 | Sept. 10, 1963 |
| Mauritius | Sept. 23, 1968 | Sept. 23, 1968 |
| [1] Mexico | Dec. 31, 1945 | Dec. 31, 1945 |
| Morocco | Apr. 25, 1958 | Apr. 25, 1958 |
| Nepal | Sept. 6, 1961 | Sept. 6, 1961 |
| [1] Netherlands | Dec. 27, 1945[3] | Dec. 26, 1945 |
| New Zealand | Aug. 31, 1961 | Aug. 31, 1961 |
| [2] Nicaragua | Mar. 14, 1946 | Mar. 14, 1946 |
| Niger | Apr. 24, 1963 | Apr. 24, 1963 |
| Nigeria | Mar. 30, 1961 | Mar. 30, 1961 |
| [1] Norway | Dec. 27, 1945 | Dec. 27, 1945 |
| Pakistan | July 11, 1950 | July 11, 1950 |
| [2] Panama | Mar. 14, 1946 | Mar. 14, 1946 |
| [1] Paraguay | Dec. 27, 1945 | Dec. 28, 1945[3] |
| [1] Peru | Dec. 31, 1945 | Dec. 31, 1945 |
| [1] Philippines | Dec. 27, 1945[3] | Dec. 21, 1945 |
| [1, 4] (Poland) | (Dec. 27, 1945) | (Jan. 10, 1946)[3] |

| Government of | Date of Signature of Articles of Agreement | Date of Deposit of Instrument of Acceptance |
|---|---|---|
| Portugal | Mar. 29, 1961 | Mar. 29, 1961 |
| Rwanda | Sept. 30, 1963 | Sept. 30, 1963 |
| Saudi Arabia | Aug. 26, 1957 | Aug. 26, 1957 |
| Senegal | Aug. 31, 1962 | Aug. 31, 1962 |
| Sierra Leone | Sept. 10, 1962 | Sept. 10, 1962 |
| Singapore | Aug. 3, 1966 | Aug. 3, 1966 |
| Somalia | Aug. 31, 1962 | Aug. 31, 1962 |
| [1] South Africa | Dec. 27, 1945[3] | Dec. 26, 1945 |
| Spain | Sept. 15, 1958 | Sept. 15, 1958 |
| Sudan | Sept. 5, 1957 | Sept. 5, 1957 |
| Sweden | Aug. 31, 1951 | Aug. 31, 1951 |
| Syrian Arab Republic | Apr. 10, 1947 | Apr. 10, 1947 |
| Tanzania | Sept. 10, 1962 | Sept. 10, 1962 |
| Thailand | May 3, 1949 | May 3, 1949 |
| Togo | Aug. 1, 1962 | Aug. 1, 1962 |
| Trinidad and Tobago | Sept. 16, 1963 | Sept. 16, 1963 |
| Tunisia | Apr. 14, 1958 | Apr. 14, 1958 |
| Turkey | Mar. 11, 1947 | Mar. 11, 1947 |
| Uganda | Sept. 27, 1963 | Sept. 27, 1963 |
| [1] United Arab Republic | Dec. 27, 1945[3] | Dec. 26, 1945 |
| [1] United Kingdom of Great Britain and Northern Ireland | Dec. 27, 1945 | Dec. 27, 1945 |
| [1] United States | Dec. 27, 1945[3] | Dec. 20, 1945 |
| Upper Volta | May 2, 1963 | May 2, 1963 |
| [1] Uruguay | Dec. 27, 1945 | Mar. 11, 1946[3] |
| [2] Venezuela | Dec. 30, 1946 | Dec. 30, 1946 |
| Viet-Nam | Sept. 21, 1956 | Sept. 21, 1956 |
| [1] Yugoslavia | Dec. 27, 1945[3] | Dec. 26, 1945 |
| Zambia | Sept. 23, 1965 | Sept. 23, 1965 |

[1] "Original members" (Article II, Section 1), which signed the Articles of Agreement by December 31, 1945.

[2] Countries that joined the Fund under the provisions for original members as extended to December 31, 1946 by Board of Governors Resolution No. IM-9.

[3] In cases where the dates of signature of the Articles of Agreement and of deposit of the instrument of acceptance for a member differ, the later date is considered the effective date of membership.

[4] Cuba withdrew from the Fund, effective April 2, 1964; Czechoslovakia ceased to be a member of the Fund, effective December 31, 1954; Poland withdrew from the Fund, effective March 14, 1950.

[5] Indonesia became a member of the Fund on April 15, 1954 and withdrew from membership, effective August 17, 1965; Indonesia was readmitted as a member of the Fund on February 21, 1967.

# APPENDIX II

## INTERNATIONAL MONETARY FUND DIRECTORY

MEMBERS, QUOTAS, GOVERNORS, VOTING POWER,

EXECUTIVE BOARD, OFFICERS

## (November 1, 1968)

| Member | QUOTA Amount (*Millions of U.S. dollars*) | Per Cent of Total | Governor *Alternate* | VOTES Number[1] | Per Cent of Total |
|---|---|---|---|---|---|
| Afghanistan | 29.00 | 0.14 | Habibullah Mali Achaczai *G. Faruq Achikzad* | 540 | 0.23 |
| Algeria | 69.00 | 0.33 | Seghir Mostefai *Yahia Khellif* | 940 | 0.39 |
| Argentina | 350.00 | 1.65 | Adalbert Krieger Vasena *Pedro Eduardo Real* | 3,750 | 1.56 |
| Australia | 500.00 | 2.36 | William McMahon *Sir Richard Randall* | 5,250 | 2.19 |
| Austria | 175.00 | 0.83 | Wolfgang Schmitz *Ludwig Seiberl* | 2,000 | 0.83 |
| Belgium | 422.00 | 1.99 | Hubert Ansiaux *M. D'Haeze* | 4,470 | 1.86 |
| Bolivia | 29.00 | 0.14 | Manuel Soria Galvarro *Wenceslao Alba Quiróz* | 540 | 0.23 |
| Botswana | 3.00 | 0.01 | M. K. Segokgo *S. W. Assael* | 280 | 0.12 |
| Brazil | 350.00 | 1.65 | Antonio Delfim Netto *Ernane Galvêas* | 3,750 | 1.56 |
| Burma | 48.00 | 0.23 | Kyaw Nyein *Tin Tun* | 730 | 0.30 |
| Burundi | 15.00 | 0.07 | Joseph Hicuburundi *Ferdinand Bitariho* | 400 | 0.17 |
| Cameroon | 17.40 | 0.08 | Bernard Bidias à Ngon *Paul Denis Mbog* | 424 | 0.18 |
| Canada | 740.00 | 3.49 | Edgar John Benson *Louis Rasminsky* | 7,650 | 3.19 |
| Central African Republic | 9.00 | 0.04 | Antoine Guimali *Joseph Moutou Mondziaou* | 340 | 0.14 |
| Ceylon | 78.00 | 0.37 | U. B. Wanninayake *William Tennekoon* | 1,030 | 0.43 |
| Chad | 9.00 | 0.04 | Abakar Sanga Traoré *René Roustan* | 340 | 0.14 |
| Chile | 125.00 | 0.59 | Carlos Massad Abud *Jorge Marshall Silva* | 1,500 | 0.63 |
| China | 550.00 | 2.59 | Peh-Yuan Hsu *Kan Lee* | 5,750 | 2.40 |
| Colombia | 125.00 | 0.59 | Eduardo Arias Robledo *Germán Botero de los Ríos* | 1,500 | 0.63 |

## MEMBERS, QUOTAS, GOVERNORS AND VOTING POWER

| | QUOTA | | | VOTES | |
|---|---|---|---|---|---|
| Member | Amount (*Millions of U.S. dollars*) | Per Cent of Total | Governor *Alternate* | Number[1] | Per Cent of Total |
| Congo (Brazzaville) | 9.00 | 0.04 | Edouard Ebouka-Babackas *Corentin Kouangha* | 340 | 0.14 |
| Congo, Democratic Republic of | 57.00 | 0.27 | Albert Ndele *Cyrille Adoula* | 820 | 0.34 |
| Costa Rica | 25.00 | 0.12 | Omar Dengo O. *Alvaro Vargas* | 500 | 0.21 |
| Cyprus | 20.00 | 0.09 | C. C. Stephani *K. Lazarides* | 450 | 0.19 |
| Dahomey | 9.00 | 0.04 | Mamadou N'Diaye *Gilles-Florent Yehouessi* | 340 | 0.14 |
| Denmark | 163.00 | 0.77 | Erik Hoffmeyer *Erik Ib Schmidt* | 1,880 | 0.78 |
| Dominican Republic | 29.20 | 0.14 | Diógenes H. Fernández *Luis M. Guerrero G.* | 542 | 0.23 |
| Ecuador | 25.00 | 0.12 | Jorge Pareja Martínez *Vacant* | 500 | 0.21 |
| El Salvador | 25.00 | 0.12 | Alfonso Moisés Beatriz *Roberto Palomo h.* | 500 | 0.21 |
| Ethiopia | 19.00 | 0.09 | Menasse Lemma *Yawand-Wossen Mangasha* | 440 | 0.18 |
| Finland | 125.00 | 0.59 | Reino Rossi *Klaus Waris* | 1,500 | 0.63 |
| France | 985.00 | 4.65 | Jacques Brunet *René Larre* | 10,100 | 4.21 |
| Gabon | 9.00 | 0.04 | Augustin Boumah *Claude Panouillot* | 340 | 0.14 |
| Gambia, The | 5.00 | 0.02 | S. M. Dibba *J. B. de Loynes* | 300 | 0.13 |
| Germany | 1,200.00 | 5.66 | Karl Blessing *Johann Schöllhorn* | 12,250 | 5.11 |
| Ghana | 69.00 | 0.33 | J. H. Frimpong-Ansah *S. E. Arthur* | 940 | 0.39 |
| Greece | 100.00 | 0.47 | Demetrius Galanis *Costas Thanos* | 1,250 | 0.52 |
| Guatemala | 25.00 | 0.12 | Francisco Fernández Rivas *Mario Fuentes Pieruccini* | 500 | 0.21 |
| Guinea | 19.00 | 0.09 | Balla Camara *N'Faly Sangaré* | 440 | 0.18 |

## MEMBERS, QUOTAS, GOVERNORS AND VOTING POWER

| Member | QUOTA Amount (*Millions of* U.S. *dollars*) | Per Cent of Total | Governor *Alternate* | VOTES Number[1] | Per Cent of Total |
|---|---|---|---|---|---|
| Guyana | 15.00 | 0.07 | W. P. D'Andrade *P. E. Matthews* | 400 | 0.17 |
| Haiti | 15.00 | 0.07 | Antonio André *Clovis Desinor* | 400 | 0.17 |
| Honduras | 19.00 | 0.09 | Roberto Ramírez *Guillermo Bueso* | 440 | 0.18 |
| Iceland | 15.00 | 0.07 | Jóhannes Nordal *Jónas Haralz* | 400 | 0.17 |
| India | 750.00 | 3.54 | Morarji R. Desai *L. K. Jha* | 7,750 | 3.23 |
| Indonesia | 207.00 | 0.98 | Radius Prawiro *Salamun Alfian Tjakradiwirja* | 2,320 | 0.97 |
| Iran | 125.00 | 0.59 | Mehdi Samii *Khodadad Farmanfarmaian* | 1,500 | 0.63 |
| Iraq | 80.00 | 0.38 | Saleh Kubba *Subhi Frankool* | 1,050 | 0.44 |
| Ireland | 80.00 | 0.38 | Charles J. Haughey *Maurice Moynihan* | 1,050 | 0.44 |
| Israel | 90.00 | 0.42 | Pinhas Sapir *Y. J. Taub* | 1,150 | 0.48 |
| Italy | 625.00 | 2.95 | Emilio Colombo *Guido Carli* | 6,500 | 2.71 |
| Ivory Coast | 17.40 | 0.08 | Konan Bédié *Jean-Baptiste Améthier* | 424 | 0.18 |
| Jamaica | 30.00 | 0.14 | Edward Seaga *G. A. Brown* | 550 | 0.23 |
| Japan | 725.00 | 3.42 | Mikio Mizuta *Makoto Usami* | 7,500 | 3.13 |
| Jordan | 16.00 | 0.08 | Khalil Salim *Rashad El-Hassan* | 410 | 0.17 |
| Kenya | 32.00 | 0.15 | J. S. Gichuru *Duncan Nderitu Ndegwa* | 570 | 0.24 |
| Korea | 50.00 | 0.24 | Jong Ryul Whang *Chin Soo Suh* | 750 | 0.31 |
| Kuwait | 50.00 | 0.24 | Abdul Rahman Salim Al-Ateeqi *Hamzah Abbas Hussein* | 750 | 0.31 |
| Laos | 7.50 | 0.04 | Sisouk Na Champassak *Oudong Souvannavong* | 325 | 0.14 |

## MEMBERS, QUOTAS, GOVERNORS AND VOTING POWER

| Member | QUOTA Amount (*Millions of U.S. dollars*) | Per Cent of Total | Governor *Alternate* | VOTES Number[1] | Per Cent of Total |
|---|---|---|---|---|---|
| Lebanon | 9.00 | 0.04 | Joseph Oughourlian *Farid Solh* | 340 | 0.14 |
| Lesotho | 3.00 | 0.01 | P. N. Peete *A. Collings* | 280 | 0.12 |
| Liberia | 20.00 | 0.09 | J. Milton Weeks *Frank J. Stewart* | 450 | 0.19 |
| Libya | 19.00 | 0.09 | Khalil Bennani *Faraj Bugrara* | 440 | 0.18 |
| Luxembourg | 17.40 | 0.08 | Pierre Werner *Pierre Guill* | 424 | 0.18 |
| Malagasy Republic | 19.00 | 0.09 | Victor Miadana *Raymond Rabenoro* | 440 | 0.18 |
| Malawi | 11.25 | 0.05 | J. Z. U. Tembo *D. Thomson* | 362 | 0.15 |
| Malaysia | 115.00 | 0.54 | Tan Siew Sin *Ismail bin Mohamed Ali* | 1,400 | 0.58 |
| Mali | 17.00 | 0.08 | Louis Nègre *Aly Cissé* | 420 | 0.18 |
| Malta | 10.00 | 0.05 | Giovanni Felice *Ph. Hogg* | 350 | 0.15 |
| Mauritania | 9.00 | 0.04 | Sidi Mohamed Diagana *Pierre Braemer* | 340 | 0.14 |
| Mauritius | 16.00 | 0.08 | Veerasamy Ringadoo *Aunauth Beejadhur* | 410 | 0.17 |
| Mexico | 270.00 | 1.27 | Antonio Ortiz Mena *Rodrigo Gómez* | 2,950 | 1.23 |
| Morocco | 82.80 | 0.39 | M'Hamed Zeghari *M'Hamed Bargach* | 1,078 | 0.45 |
| Nepal | 10.00 | 0.05 | Yadav Prasad Pant *Kumar Mani Dikshit* | 350 | 0.15 |
| Netherlands | 520.00 | 2.45 | J. Zijlstra *E. van Lennep* | 5,450 | 2.27 |
| New Zealand | 157.00 | 0.74 | R. D. Muldoon *R. W. R. White* | 1,820 | 0.76 |
| Nicaragua | 19.00 | 0.09 | Gustavo Guerrero *José María Castillo* | 440 | 0.18 |
| Niger | 9.00 | 0.04 | Courmo Barcourgné *Charles Godefroy* | 340 | 0.14 |

| | QUOTA | | | VOTES | |
|---|---|---|---|---|---|
| Member | Amount (*Millions of U.S. dollars*) | Per Cent of Total | Governor *Alternate* | Number[1] | Per Cent of Total |
| Nigeria | 100.00 | 0.47 | O. Awolowo *C. N. Isong* | 1,250 | 0.52 |
| Norway | 150.00 | 0.71 | Erik Brofoss *Thomas Løvold* | 1,750 | 0.73 |
| Pakistan | 188.00 | 0.89 | M. Raschid *M. Majid Ali* | 2,130 | 0.89 |
| Panama | 11.25 | 0.05 | Jorge T. Velásquez *Héctor Marciaq* | 362 | 0.15 |
| Paraguay | 15.00 | 0.07 | César Barrientos *Edgar F. Taboada* | 400 | 0.17 |
| Peru | 85.00 | 0.40 | Celso Pastor *Emilio G. Barreto* | 1,100 | 0.46 |
| Philippines | 110.00 | 0.52 | Alfonso Calalang *Roberto S. Benedicto* | 1,350 | 0.56 |
| Portugal | 75.00 | 0.35 | António Manuel Pinto Barbosa *Manuel Jacinto Nunes* | 1,000 | 0.42 |
| Rwanda | 15.00 | 0.07 | Masaya Hattori *Jean Birara* | 400 | 0.17 |
| Saudi Arabia | 90.00 | 0.42 | Ahmed Zaki Saad *Abid M. S. Sheikh* | 1,150 | 0.48 |
| Senegal | 25.00 | 0.12 | Jean Collin *Louis Jean Eude* | 500 | 0.21 |
| Sierra Leone | 15.00 | 0.07 | M. S. Forna *S. B. Nicol-Cole* | 400 | 0.17 |
| Singapore | 30.00 | 0.14 | Goh Keng Swee *Hon Sui Sen* | 550 | 0.23 |
| Somalia | 15.00 | 0.07 | Abdullahi Ahmed Addou *Ali Issa Farah* | 400 | 0.17 |
| South Africa | 200.00 | 0.94 | Nicolaas Diederichs *G. W. G. Browne* | 2,250 | 0.94 |
| Spain | 250.00 | 1.18 | Faustino García Moncó *Manuel Varela* | 2,750 | 1.15 |
| Sudan | 57.00 | 0.27 | El Sherif Hussein El Hindi *Abdel Rahim Mirghani* | 820 | 0.34 |
| Sweden | 225.00 | 1.06 | Per V. Åsbrink *S. F. Joge* | 2,500 | 1.04 |
| Syrian Arab Republic | 38.00 | 0.18 | Zouhair Kani *Adnan Farra* | 630 | 0.26 |

## MEMBERS, QUOTAS, GOVERNORS AND VOTING POWER

| Member | QUOTA Amount (*Millions of U.S. dollars*) | Per Cent of Total | Governor *Alternate* | VOTES Number[1] | Per Cent of Total |
|---|---|---|---|---|---|
| Tanzania | 32.00 | 0.15 | A. H. Jamal *E. I. M. Mtei* | 570 | 0.24 |
| Thailand | 95.00 | 0.45 | Puey Ungphakorn *Boonma Wongswan* | 1,200 | 0.50 |
| Togo | 11.25 | 0.05 | Paulin Eklou *Edouard Kodjo* | 362 | 0.15 |
| Trinidad and Tobago | 44.00 | 0.21 | F. C. Prevatt *A. N. McLeod* | 690 | 0.29 |
| Tunisia | 35.00 | 0.17 | Hédi Nouira *Abderrazak Rassaa* | 600 | 0.25 |
| Turkey | 108.00 | 0.51 | Fahir Tigrel *Naim Talu* | 1,330 | 0.55 |
| Uganda | 32.00 | 0.15 | L. Kalule-Settala *J. M. Mubiru* | 570 | 0.24 |
| United Arab Republic | 150.00 | 0.71 | A. Nazmy Abdel Hamid *Mahmoud Sedky Mourad* | 1,750 | 0.73 |
| United Kingdom | 2,440.00 | 11.51 | Roy Jenkins *C. J. Morse* | 24,650 | 10.28 |
| United States | 5,160.00 | 24.34 | Henry H. Fowler *Eugene V. Rostow* | 51,850 | 21.63 |
| Upper Volta | 9.00 | 0.04 | Tiémoko Marc Garango *Robert Pebayle* | 340 | 0.14 |
| Uruguay | 55.00 | 0.26 | Enrique V. Iglesias *Juan M. Bracco* | 800 | 0.33 |
| Venezuela | 250.00 | 1.18 | Benito Raúl Losado *Carlos González Naranjo* | 2,750 | 1.15 |
| Viet-Nam | 39.00 | 0.18 | Nguyên Huu Hanh *Nguyên Van Dong* | 640 | 0.27 |
| Yugoslavia | 150.00 | 0.71 | Kiro Gligorov *Nikola Miljanic* | 1,750 | 0.73 |
| Zambia | 50.00 | 0.24 | Elijah H. K. Mudenda *J. B. Zulu* | 750 | 0.31 |
| | 21,198.45 | 100.00[2] | | 239,733 | 100.00[2] |

[1] Voting power varies on certain matters with use by members of the Fund's resources.
[2] This figure may differ from the sum of the percentages shown for individual countries because of rounding.

| Director<br>*Alternate* | Casting<br>Votes of | Votes by<br>Country | Total<br>Votes[1] | Per Cent<br>of Total |
|---|---|---|---|---|
| **APPOINTED** | | | | |
| William B. Dale<br>*John S. Hooker* | United States | 51,850 | 51,850 | 22.12 |
| E. W. Maude<br>*Guy Huntrods* | United Kingdom | 24,650 | 24,650 | 10.52 |
| Guenther Schleiminger<br>*Lore Fuenfgelt* | Germany | 12,250 | 12,250 | 5.23 |
| Georges Plescoff<br>*Bruno de Maulde* | France | 10,100 | 10,100 | 4.31 |
| B. K. Madan<br>*Arun K. Banerji* | India | 7,750 | 7,750 | 3.31 |
| Francesco Palamenghi-Crispi<br>*Carlos Bustelo (Spain)* | Italy[2] | 6,500 | 6,500 | 2.77 |
| **ELECTED** | | | | |
| Ahmed Zaki Saad<br>(United Arab Republic)<br>*Vacant* | Afghanistan<br>Ethiopia<br>Iran<br>Iraq<br>Jordan<br>Kuwait<br>Lebanon<br>Pakistan<br>Philippines<br>Saudi Arabia<br>Somalia<br>Syrian Arab Republic<br>United Arab Republic | 540<br>440<br>1,500<br>1,050<br>410<br>750<br>340<br>2,130<br>1,350<br>1,150<br>400<br>630<br>1,750 | 12,440 | 5.31 |
| Hideo Suzuki (Japan)<br>*Seitaro Hattori (Japan)* | Burma<br>Ceylon<br>Japan<br>Nepal<br>Thailand | 730<br>1,030<br>7,500<br>350<br>1,200 | 10,810 | 4.61 |
| Robert Johnstone (Canada)<br>*Maurice Horgan (Ireland)* | Canada<br>Guyana<br>Ireland<br>Jamaica | 7,650<br>400<br>1,050<br>550 | 9,650 | 4.12 |
| J. O. Stone (Australia)<br>*G. P. C. de Kock (South Africa)* | Australia<br>Lesotho<br>New Zealand<br>South Africa | 5,250<br>280<br>1,820<br>2,250 | 9,600 | 4.10 |

*86*

| Director<br>*Alternate* | Casting<br>Votes of | Votes by<br>Country | Total<br>Votes[1] | Per Cent<br>of Total |
|---|---|---|---|---|
| **ELECTED** (Continued) | | | | |
| Pieter Lieftinck (Netherlands) | Cyprus | 450 | | |
| *H. M. H. A. van der Valk* | Israel | 1,150 | | |
| *(Netherlands)* | Netherlands | 5,450 | | |
| | Yugoslavia | 1,750 | 8,800 | 3.75 |
| | | | | |
| Byanti Kharmawan (Indonesia) | Algeria | 940 | | |
| *Abdoel Hamid (Indonesia)* | Ghana | 940 | | |
| | Indonesia | 2,320 | | |
| | Laos | 325 | | |
| | Libya | 440 | | |
| | Malaysia | 1,400 | | |
| | Morocco | 1,078 | | |
| | Singapore | 550 | | |
| | Tunisia | 600 | 8,593 | 3.67 |
| | | | | |
| Leonard A. Williams (Trinidad | Botswana | 280 | | |
| and Tobago) | Burundi | 400 | | |
| *Maurice Peter Omwony (Kenya)* | Gambia, The | 300 | | |
| | Guinea | 440 | | |
| | Kenya | 570 | | |
| | Liberia | 450 | | |
| | Malawi | 362 | | |
| | Mali | 420 | | |
| | Nigeria | 1,250 | | |
| | Sierra Leone | 400 | | |
| | Sudan | 820 | | |
| | Tanzania | 570 | | |
| | Trinidad and Tobago | 690 | | |
| | Uganda | 570 | | |
| | Zambia | 750 | 8,272 | 3.53 |
| | | | | |
| André van Campenhout (Belgium) | Austria | 2,000 | | |
| *Herman Biron (Belgium)* | Belgium | 4,470 | | |
| | Luxembourg | 424 | | |
| | Turkey | 1,330 | 8,224 | 3.51 |
| | | | | |
| Alfredo Phillips O. (Mexico) | Costa Rica | 500 | | |
| *Marcos A. Sandoval (Venezuela)* | El Salvador | 500 | | |
| | Guatemala | 500 | | |
| | Honduras | 440 | | |
| | Mexico | 2,950 | | |
| | Nicaragua | 440 | | |
| | Venezuela | 2,750 | 8,080 | 3.45 |
| | | | | |
| Eero Asp (Finland) | Denmark | 1,880 | | |
| *Jorma Aranko (Finland)* | Finland | 1,500 | | |
| | Iceland | 400 | | |
| | Norway | 1,750 | | |
| | Sweden | 2,500 | 8,030 | 3.43 |

*87*

| Director<br>*Alternate* | Casting<br>Votes of | Votes by<br>Country | Total<br>Votes[1] | Per Cent<br>of Total |
|---|---|---|---|---|
| **ELECTED** (Continued) | | | | |
| Alexandre Kafka (Brazil)<br>*Eduardo da S. Gomes, Jr. (Brazil)* | Brazil<br>Colombia<br>Dominican Republic<br>Haiti<br>Panama<br>Peru | 3,750<br>1,500<br>542<br>400<br>362<br>1,100 | 7,654 | 3.27 |
| Luis Escobar (Chile)<br>*Ricardo H. Arriazu (Argentina)* | Argentina<br>Bolivia<br>Chile<br>Ecuador<br>Paraguay<br>Uruguay | 3,750<br>540<br>1,500<br>500<br>400<br>800 | 7,490 | 3.20 |
| Beue Tann (China)<br>*Nguyên Huu Hanh (Viet-Nam)* | China<br>Korea<br>Viet-Nam | 5,750<br>750<br>640 | 7,140 | 3.05 |
| Antoine W. Yaméogo<br>(Upper Volta)<br>*Léon M. Rajaobelina*<br>*(Malagasy Republic)* | Cameroon<br>Central African Republic<br>Chad<br>Congo (Brazzaville)<br>Congo, Democratic Rep. of<br>Dahomey<br>Gabon<br>Ivory Coast<br>Malagasy Republic<br>Mauritania<br>Mauritius<br>Niger<br>Rwanda<br>Senegal<br>Togo<br>Upper Volta | 424<br>340<br>340<br>340<br>820<br>340<br>340<br>424<br>440<br>340<br>410<br>340<br>400<br>500<br>362<br>340 | 6,500 | 2.77 |
| | | | 234,383[2] | 100.00[3] |

[1] Voting power varies on certain matters with use by members of the Fund's resources.
[2] This total does not include the votes of Greece, Malta, Portugal, and Spain, which did not participate in the 1968 Regular Election of Executive Directors. These members have designated the Executive Director appointed by Italy to look after their interests in the Fund.
[3] This figure may differ from the sum of the percentages shown for individual countries because of rounding.

## OFFICERS OF THE INTERNATIONAL MONETARY FUND
19th and H Streets, N.W., Washington, D.C. 20431

Managing Director.................................Pierre-Paul Schweitzer
Deputy Managing Director..........................Frank A. Southard, Jr.
The General Counsel................................Joseph Gold
The Economic Counsellor............................J. J. Polak
Administration Department
   Director.......................................Phillip Thorson
African Department
   Director.......................................Mamoudou Touré
Asian Department
   Director.......................................D. S. Savkar
Central Banking Service
   Director.......................................J. V. Mládek
European Department
   Director.......................................L. A. Whittome
Exchange and Trade Relations Department
   Director.......................................Ernest Sturc
Fiscal Affairs Department
   Director.......................................Richard Goode
IMF Institute
   Director.......................................F. A. G. Keesing
Legal Department
   Director.......................................Joseph Gold
Middle Eastern Department
   Acting Director*...............................John W. Gunter
Research Department
   Director.......................................J. J. Polak
Secretary's Department
   Secretary......................................W. Lawrence Hebbard
Treasurer's Department
   Treasurer......................................Oscar L. Altman
Western Hemisphere Department
   Director.......................................Jorge Del Canto
Bureau of Statistics
   Director.......................................Earl Hicks
Office in Europe (Paris)
   Director.......................................Jean-Paul Sallé
Office in Geneva
   Director.......................................Edgar Jones
Chief Information Officer...........................Jay Reid
Internal Auditor...................................J. William Lowe
Special Representative to the United Nations...........Gordon Williams

---

\* Anwar Ali, Director (on leave)

# APPENDIX III

## SCHEDULE-A QUOTAS

[In millions of United States dollars]

| | | | |
|---|---|---|---|
| Australia | 200 | Iran | 25 |
| Belgium | 225 | Iraq | 8 |
| Bolivia | 10 | Liberia | .5 |
| Brazil | 150 | Luxembourg | 10 |
| Canada | 300 | Mexico | 90 |
| Chile | 50 | Netherlands | 275 |
| China | 550 | New Zealand | 50 |
| Colombia | 50 | Nicaragua | 2 |
| Costa Rica | 5 | Norway | 50 |
| Cuba | 50 | Panama | .5 |
| Czechoslovakia | 125 | Paraguay | 2 |
| Denmark | (1) | Peru | 25 |
| Dominican Republic | 5 | Philippine Common- | |
| Ecuador | 5 | wealth | 15 |
| Egypt | 45 | Poland | 125 |
| El Salvador | 2.5 | Union of South Africa | 100 |
| Ethiopia | 6 | Union of Soviet Socialist | |
| France | 450 | Republics | 1,200 |
| Greece | 40 | United Kingdom | 1,300 |
| Guatemala | 5 | United States | 2,750 |
| Haiti | 5 | Uruguay | 15 |
| Honduras | 2.5 | Venezuela | 15 |
| Iceland | 1 | Yugoslavia | 60 |
| India | 400 | | |
| | | Total | 8,800 |

[1] The quota of Denmark shall be determined by the Fund after the Danish Government has declared its readiness to sign this Agreement but before signature takes place.

# PUBLICATIONS OF THE
# INTERNATIONAL FINANCE SECTION

The International Finance Section publishes at irregular intervals papers in four series: ESSAYS IN INTERNATIONAL FINANCE, PRINCETON STUDIES IN INTERNATIONAL FINANCE, SPECIAL PAPERS IN INTERNATIONAL ECONOMICS, and REPRINTS IN INTERNATIONAL FINANCE. All four of these should be ordered directly from the Section (P.O. Box 644, Princeton, New Jersey 08540).

A mailing list is maintained for free distribution of ESSAYS and REPRINTS as they are issued and of announcements of new issues in the series of STUDIES and SPECIAL PAPERS. Requests for inclusion in this list will be honored, except that students will not be placed on the permanent mailing list, because waste results from frequent changes of address.

For the STUDIES and SPECIAL PAPERS there will be a charge of $1.00 a copy, payable in advance. This charge will be waived on copies distributed to college and university libraries here and abroad. In addition the charge is sometimes waived on single copies requested by persons residing abroad who find it difficult to make remittance.

For noneducational institutions there is a simplified procedure whereby all issues of all four series will be sent to them automatically in return for an annual contribution of $25 to the publication program of the International Finance Section. Any company finding it irksome to order individual SPECIAL PAPERS and STUDIES is welcome to take advantage of this plan.

Orders for single copies of the ESSAYS and REPRINTS will be filled against a handling charge of $1.00, payable in advance. The charge for more than one copy of these two series will be $0.50 a copy. These charges may be waived to foreign institutions of education and research. Charges may also be waived on single copies requested by persons residing abroad who find it difficult to make remittance.

For the convenience of our British customers, arrangements have been made for retail distribution of the STUDIES and SPECIAL PAPERS through the Economists' Bookshop, Portugal Street, London, W.C. 2, and Blackwells, Broad Street, Oxford. These booksellers will usually have our publications in stock.

The following is a complete list of the publications of the International Finance Section. The issues of the four series that are still available from the Section are marked by asterisks. Those marked by daggers are out of stock at the International Finance Section but may be obtained in xerographic reproductions (that is, looking like the originals) from University Microfilm, Inc., 300 N. Zeeb Road, Ann Arbor, Michigan 48106. (Most of the issues are priced at $3.00.)

†No. 1. Friedrich A. Lutz, *International Monetary Mechanisms: The Keynes and White Proposals*. (July 1943)
† 2. Frank D. Graham, *Fundamentals of International Monetary Policy*. (Autumn 1943)
† 3. Richard A. Lester, *International Aspects of Wartime Monetary Experience*. (Aug. 1944)
† 4. Ragnar Nurkse, *Conditions of International Monetary Equilibrium*. (Spring 1945)
† 5. Howard S. Ellis, *Bilateralism and the Future of International Trade*. (Summer 1945)
† 6. Arthur I. Bloomfield, *The British Balance-of-Payments Problem*. (Autumn 1945)
† 7. Frank A. Southard, Jr., *Some European Currency and Exchange Experiences: 1943-1946*. (Summer 1946)
† 8. Miroslav A. Kriz, *Postwar International Lending*. (Spring 1947)
† 9. Friedrich A. Lutz, *The Marshall Plan and European Economic Policy*. (Spring 1948)
† 10. Frank D. Graham, *The Cause and Cure of "Dollar Shortage."* (Jan. 1949)
† 11. Horst Mendershausen, *Dollar Shortage and Oil Surplus in 1949-1950*. (Nov. 1950)
† 12. Sir Arthur Salter, *Foreign Investment*. (Feb. 1951)
† 13. Sir Roy Harrod, *The Pound Sterling*. (Feb. 1952)
† 14. S. Herbert Frankel, *Some Conceptual Aspects of International Economic Development of Underdeveloped Territories*. (May 1952)
† 15. Miroslav A. Kriz, *The Price of Gold*. (July 1952)
† 16. William Diebold, Jr., *The End of the I.T.O.* (Oct. 1952)
† 17. Sir Douglas Copland, *Problems of the Sterling Area: With Special Reference to Australia*. (Sept. 1953)
† 18. Raymond F. Mikesell, *The Emerging Pattern of International Payments*. (April 1954)
† 19. D. Gale Johnson, *Agricultural Price Policy and International Trade*. (June 1954)
† 20. Ida Greaves, *"The Colonial Sterling Balances."* (Sept. 1954)
† 21. Raymond Vernon, *America's Foreign Trade Policy and the GATT*. (Oct. 1954)
† 22. Roger Auboin, *The Bank for International Settlements, 1930-1955*. (May 1955)
† 23. Wytze Gorter, *United States Merchant Marine Policies: Some International Implications*. (June 1955)
† 24. Thomas C. Schelling, *International Cost-Sharing Arrangements*. (Sept. 1955)
† 25. James E. Meade, *The Belgium-Luxembourg Economic Union, 1921-1939*. (March 1956)
† 26. Samuel I. Katz, *Two Approaches to the Exchange-Rate Problem: The United Kingdom and Canada*. (Aug. 1956)
† 27. A. R. Conan, *The Changing Pattern of International Investment in Selected Sterling Countries*. (Dec. 1956)
† 28. Fred H. Klopstock, *The International Status of the Dollar*. (May 1957)
† 29. Raymond Vernon, *Trade Policy in Crisis*. (March 1958)
† 30. Sir Roy Harrod, *The Pound Sterling, 1951-1958*. (Aug. 1958)
† 31. Randall Hinshaw, *Toward European Convertibility*. (Nov. 1958)
† 32. Francis H. Schott, *The Evolution of Latin American Exchange-Rate Policies since World War II*. (Jan. 1959)
† 33. Alec Cairncross, *The International Bank for Reconstruction and Development*. (March 1959)
† 34. Miroslav A. Kriz, *Gold in World Monetary Affairs Today*. (June 1959)

† 35. Sir Donald MacDougall, *The Dollar Problem: A Reappraisal.* (Nov. 1960)

† 36. Brian Tew, *The International Monetary Fund: Its Present Role and Future Prospect.* (March 1961)

† 37. Samuel I. Katz, *Sterling Speculation and European Convertibility: 1955-1958.* (Oct. 1961)

† 38. Boris C. Swerling, *Current Issues in International Commodity Policy.* (June 1962)

† 39. Pieter Lieftinck, *Recent Trends in International Monetary Policies.* (Sept. 1962)

† 40. Jerome L. Stein, *The Nature and Efficiency of the Foreign Exchange Market.* (Oct. 1962)

† 41. Friedrich A. Lutz, *The Problem of International Liquidity and the Multiple-Currency Standard.* (March 1963)

† 42. Sir Dennis Robertson, *A Memorandum Submitted to the Canadian Royal Commission on Banking and Finance.* (May 1963)

† 43. Marius W. Holtrop, *Monetary Policy in an Open Economy: Its Objectives, Instruments, Limitations, and Dilemmas.* (Sept. 1963)

† 44. Harry G. Johnson, *Alternative Guiding Principles for the Use of Monetary Policy.* (Nov. 1963)

† 45. Jacob Viner, *Problems of Monetary Control.* (May 1964)

† 46. Charles P. Kindleberger, *Balance-of-Payments Deficits and the International Market for Liquidity.* (May 1965)

† 47. Jacques Rueff and Fred Hirsch, *The Role and the Rule of Gold: An Argument.* (June 1965)

† 48. Sidney Weintraub, *The Foreign-Exchange Gap of the Developing Countries.* (Sept. 1965)

† 49. Tibor Scitovsky, *Requirements of an International Reserve System.* (Nov. 1965)

† 50. John H. Williamson, *The Crawling Peg.* (Dec. 1965)

† 51. Pieter Lieftinck, *External Debt and Debt-Bearing Capacity of Developing Countries.* (March 1966)

† 52. Raymond F. Mikesell, *Public Foreign Capital for Private Enterprise in Developing Countries.* (April 1966)

† 53. Milton Gilbert, *Problems of the International Monetary System.* (April 1966)

† 54. Robert V. Roosa and Fred Hirsch, *Reserves, Reserve Currencies, and Vehicle Currencies: An Argument.* (May 1966)

† 55. Robert Triffin, *The Balance of Payments and the Foreign Investment Position of the United States.* (Sept. 1966)

† 56. John Parke Young, *United States Gold Policy: The Case for Change.* (Oct. 1966)

* 57. Gunther Ruff, *A Dollar-Reserve System as a Transitional Solution.* (Jan. 1967)

* 58. J. Marcus Fleming, *Toward Assessing the Need for International Reserves.* (Feb. 1967)

* 59. N. T. Wang, *New Proposals for the International Finance of Development.* (April 1967)

† 60. Miroslav A. Kriz, *Gold: Barbarous Relic or Useful Instrument?* (June 1967)

* 61. Charles P. Kindleberger, *The Politics of International Money and World Language.* (Aug. 1967)

* 62. Delbert A. Snider, *Optimum Adjustment Processes and Currency Areas.* (Oct. 1967)

† 63. Eugene A. Birnbaum, *Changing the United States Commitment to Gold.* (Nov. 1967)

* 64. Alexander K. Swoboda, *The Euro-Dollar Market: An Interpretation.* (Feb. 1968)

* 65. Fred H. Klopstock, *The Euro-Dollar Market: Some Unresolved Issues.* (March 1968)

* 66. Eugene A. Birnbaum, *Gold and the International Monetary System: An Orderly Reform.* (April 1968)
* 67. J. Marcus Fleming, *Guidelines for Balance-of-Payments Adjustment under the Par-Value System.* (May 1968)
* 68. George N. Halm, *International Financial Intermediation: Deficits Benign and Malignant.* (June 1968)
* 69. Albert O. Hirschman and Richard M. Bird, *Foreign Aid—A Critique and a Proposal.* (July 1968)
* 70. Milton Gilbert, *The Gold-Dollar System: Conditions of Equilibrium and the Price of Gold.* (Nov. 1968)
* 71. Henry G. Aubrey, *Behind the Veil of International Money.* (Jan. 1969)
* 72. Anthony Lanyi, *The Case for Floating Exchange Rates Reconsidered.* (Feb. 1969)
* 73. George N. Halm, *Toward Limited Exchange-Rate Flexibility.* (March 1969)
* 74. Ronald I. McKinnon, *Private and Official International Money: The Case for the Dollar.* (April 1969)
* 75. Jack L. Davies, *Gold: A Forward Strategy.* (May 1969)

PRINCETON STUDIES IN INTERNATIONAL FINANCE

†No. 1. Friedrich A. and Vera C. Lutz, *Monetary and Foreign Exchange Policy in Italy.* (Jan. 1950)
† 2. Eugene R. Schlesinger, *Multiple Exchange Rates and Economic Development.* (May 1952)
† 3. Arthur I. Bloomfield, *Speculative and Flight Movements of Capital in Postwar International Finance.* (Feb. 1954)
† 4. Merlyn N. Trued and Raymond F. Mikesell, *Postwar Bilateral Payments Agreements.* (April 1955)
† 5. Derek Curtis Bok, *The First Three Years of the Schuman Plan.* (Dec. 1955)
† 6. James E. Meade, *Negotiations for Benelux: An Annotated Chronicle, 1943-1956.* (March 1957)
† 7. H. H. Liesner, *The Import Dependence of Britain and Western Germany: A Comparative Study.* (Dec. 1957)
† 8. Raymond F. Mikesell and Jack N. Behrman, *Financing Free World Trade with the Sino-Soviet Bloc.* (Sept. 1958)
† 9. Marina von Neumann Whitman, *The United States Investment Guaranty Program and Private Foreign Investment.* (Dec. 1959)
† 10. Peter B. Kenen, *Reserve-Asset Preferences of Central Banks and Stability of the Gold-Exchange Standard.* (June 1963)
* 11. Arthur I. Bloomfield, *Short-Term Capital Movements under the Pre-1914 Gold Standard.* (July 1963)
* 12. Robert Triffin, *The Evolution of the International Monetary System: Historical Reappraisal and Future Perspectives.* (June 1964)
* 13. Robert Z. Aliber, *The Management of the Dollar in International Finance.* (June 1964)
* 14. Weir M. Brown, *The External Liquidity of an Advanced Country.* (Oct. 1964)
† 15. E. Ray Canterbery, *Foreign Exchange, Capital Flows, and Monetary Policy.* (June 1965)
* 16. Ronald I. McKinnon and Wallace E. Oates, *The Implications of International Economic Integration for Monetary, Fiscal, and Exchange-Rate Policy.* (March 1966)
* 17. Egon Sohmen, *The Theory of Forward Exchange.* (Aug. 1966)
* 18. Benjamin J. Cohen, *Adjustment Costs and the Distribution of New Reserves.* (Oct. 1966)
* 19. Marina von Neumann Whitman, *International and Interregional Payments Adjustment: A Synthetic View.* (Feb. 1967)

* 20. Fred R. Glahe, *An Empirical Study of the Foreign-Exchange Market: Test of A Theory.* (June 1967)
* 21. Arthur I. Bloomfield, *Patterns of Fluctuation in International Investment Before 1914.* (Dec. 1968)
* 22. Samuel I. Katz, *External Surpluses, Capital Flows, and Credit Policy in the European Economic Community.* (Feb. 1969)
* 23. Hans Aufricht, *The Fund Agreement: Living Law and Emerging Practice.* (June 1969)

### SPECIAL PAPERS IN INTERNATIONAL ECONOMICS

*No. 1. Gottfried Haberler, *A Survey of International Trade Theory.* (Sept. 1955; Revised edition, July 1961)
† 2. Oskar Morgenstern, *The Validity of International Gold Movement Statistics.* (Nov. 1955)
* 3. Fritz Machlup, *Plans for Reform of the International Monetary System.* (Aug. 1962; Revised edition, March 1964)
† 4. Egon Sohmen, *International Monetary Problems and the Foreign Exchanges.* (April 1963)
† 5. Walther Lederer, *The Balance on Foreign Transactions: Problems of Definition and Measurement.* (Sept. 1963)
* 6. George N. Halm, *The "Band" Proposal: The Limits of Permissible Exchange Rate Variations.* (Jan. 1965)
* 7. W. M. Corden, *Recent Developments in the Theory of International Trade.* (March 1965)
* 8. Jagdish Bhagwati, *The Theory and Practice of Commercial Policy: Departures from Unified Exchange Rates.* (Jan. 1968)

### REPRINTS IN INTERNATIONAL FINANCE

†No. 1. Fritz Machlup, *The Cloakroom Rule of International Reserves: Reserve Creation and Resources Transfer.* [Reprinted from *Quarterly Journal of Economics*, Vol. LXXIX (Aug. 1965)]
† 2. Fritz Machlup, *Real Adjustment, Compensatory Corrections, and Foreign Financing of Imbalances in International Payments.* [Reprinted from Robert E. Baldwin *et al.*, *Trade, Growth, and the Balance of Payments* (Chicago: Rand McNally and Amsterdam: North-Holland Publishing Co., 1965)]
† 3. Fritz Machlup, *International Monetary Systems and the Free Market Economy.* [Reprinted from *International Payments Problems: A Symposium* (Washington, D.C.: American Enterprise Institute, 1966)]
* 4. Fritz Machlup, *World Monetary Debate—Bases for Agreement.* [Reprinted from *The Banker*, Vol. 116 (Sept. 1966)]
* 5. Fritz Machlup, *The Need for Monetary Reserves.* [Reprinted from *Banca Nazionale del Lavoro Quarterly Review*, Vol. 77 (Sept. 1966)]
* 6. Benjamin J. Cohen, *Voluntary Foreign Investment Curbs: A Plan that Really Works.* [Reprinted from *Challenge: The Magazine of Economic Affairs* (March/April 1967)]
* 7. Fritz Machlup, *Credit Facilities or Reserve Allotments?* [Reprinted from *Banca Nazionale del Lavoro Quarterly Review*, No. 81 (June 1967)]
* 8. Fritz Machlup, *From Dormant Liabilities to Dormant Assets.* [Reprinted from *The Banker*, Vol. 117 (Sept. 1967)]
* 9. Benjamin J. Cohen, *Reparations in the Postwar Period: A Survey.* [Reprinted from *Banca Nazionale del Lavoro Quarterly Review*, No. 82 (Sept. 1967)]
* 10. Fritz Machlup, *The Price of Gold.* [Reprinted from *The Banker*, Vol. 118 (Sept. 1968)]
* 11. Fritz Machlup, *The Transfer Gap of the United States.* [Reprinted from *Banca Nazionale del Lavoro Quarterly Review*, No. 86 (Sept. 1968)]

### SEPARATE PUBLICATIONS

† (1) **Klaus Knorr** and **Gardner Patterson** (editors), *A Critique of the Randall Commission Report.* (1954)

† (2) Gardner Patterson and Edgar S. Furniss Jr. (editors), *NATO: A Critical Appraisal.* (1957)

* (3) Fritz Machlup and Burton G. Malkiel (editors), *International Monetary Arrangements: The Problem of Choice.* Report on the Deliberations of an International Study Group of 32 Economists. (Aug. 1964) [$1.00]

---

AVAILABLE FROM OTHER SOURCES

William Fellner, Fritz Machlup, Robert Triffin, and Eleven Others, *Maintaining and Restoring Balance in International Payments* (1966). [This volume may be ordered from Princeton University Press, Princeton, New Jersey 08540, at a price of $6.50.]

Fritz Machlup, *Remaking the International Monetary System: The Rio Agreement and Beyond* (1968). [This volume may be ordered from the Johns Hopkins Press, Baltimore, Maryland 21218, at $6.95 in cloth cover and $2.45 in paperback.]